Volume the Second

By Jane Austen

In Her Own Hand

INTRODUCTION BY
KATHRYN SUTHERLAND

Abbeville Press Publishers
NEW YORK LONDON

EDITOR: Joan Strasbaugh
DESIGN AND TYPESETTING: Ada Rodriguez
PRODUCTION MANAGER: Louise Kurtz

First published in the United States of America in 2014 by Abbeville Press, 137 Varick Street,
New York, NY 10013

Extracts taken from *Minor Works*, Jane Austen, collected and edited from the manuscripts by
R. W. Chapman (1963) by permission of Oxford University Press.

Frontispiece reproduced by permission of Jane Austen's House Museum,
Jane Austen Memorial Trust

First edition
10 9 8 7 6 5 4 3 2 1

Library of Congress Cataloging-in-Publication Data

Austen, Jane, 1775–1817.
 [Works. Selections]
 Volume the second by Jane Austen : in her own hand / Jane Austen ; introduction by Kathryn
Sutherland. —First edition.
     pages cm. —(Jane Austen: in her own hand ; 2)
  Summary: "Volume the Second is one of three notebooks written by Jane Austen in her teens. Volume
the Second includes 3 stories and several letters and fragments she calls "scraps," all written in her own
hand. An introduction by Kathryn Sutherland and transcription are included"—Provided by publisher.
  ISBN 978-0-7892-1200-9 (hardback)
  1. Austen, Jane, 1775-1817—Manuscripts—Facsimiles. 2. Manuscripts, English—Facsimiles. I. Title. II.
Title: In her own hand.
  PR4032 2014b
  828'.709—dc23
                    2014016114

For bulk and premium sales and for text adoption procedures, write to Customer Service Manager,
Abbeville Press, 137 Varick Street, New York, NY 10013, or call 1-800-ARTBOOK.

Visit Abbeville Press online at www.abbeville.com.

CONTENTS

TEENAGE READING AND REBELLION
by Kathryn Sutherland

5

VOLUME THE SECOND

11

TRANSCRIPTION

267

Back front of Steventon Rectory. 1814

TEENAGE READING AND REBELLION

A s its mock-solemn title implies, *Volume the Second* is the second in a series of notebooks into which the teenage Jane Austen copied her early compositions. This is the most finished of the three collections; it is also the longest (with 252 pages) and the most carefully structured. Twelve leaves are missing from its original structure, five of them taken from the end, most likely removed at the time of writing into the notebook. No empty space is left, and there is no obvious development in the young author's hand to suggest that she worked on the entries over a long period. Internal dating (from June 1790 to January 1793, when her niece Fanny Austen was born) links the contents with a period of high productivity, particularly intense between the ages of fifteen and sixteen.[1]

Where the truncated fragments of *Volume the First* riot in joyous disorder, barely anchored by their network of family dedications, the pieces assembled here achieve a more unified sensibility without sacrificing any of their comedy. Indeed, *Volume the Second* has a good claim to be Jane Austen's funniest work; it is impossible not to laugh out loud while reading it. The manuscript is made up of nine items: two works identified by the author as "novels" ("Love and Freindship" and "Lesley Castle"); a spoof "History of England"; "A Collection of Letters"; and five "Scraps," among them the single act of a comic play, which conclude the volume and form a matching bookend to the mini-anthology of "Miscellanious Morsels" or "Detached peices" that round off *Volume the First*. Dedicated to her firstborn niece, Fanny Austen (as those inserted at a slightly later date into *Volume the First* are to her second niece, Anna Austen), these final sketches openly mock the restrictive educational diet proposed for young ladies and the narrow role of moral guide laid down for spinster aunts. Young Aunt Jane will have none of it; instead, the final pages of both notebooks seal a more subversive contract with the next generation of Austen females. As she writes here to Fanny, only weeks old: "I think it is my particular Duty to prevent your feeling as much as possible the want of my personal instructions, by addressing to You on paper my Opinions & Admonitions on the conduct of Young Women, which you will find expressed in the following pages" (p. 237).[2]

"Opinions & Admonitions on the conduct of Young Women" offers a good way into understanding the structure and contents of *Volume the Second*, with its sustained onslaught on the conventional limits imposed on female behavior. Other hints as to how to read the collection are provided in its repeated use of the epistolary form, and

---

Back view of STEVENTON RECTORY, where Jane Austen composed her juvenilia, by Anna Lefroy, Jane Austen's niece, 1814.

especially the novel in letters, and its focus on sensibility as a facet or modifier of behavior. The late eighteenth century saw a proliferation of works featuring heroes and heroines of sensibility; that is, characters sympathetic to the sufferings and feelings of others. Where knockabout humor dominated *Volume the First*, *Volume the Second* represents a shift towards more extended studies of character and motive. Austen's word "**conduct**" is key here, with its reference to that sector of the late-eighteenth-century book market dedicated to manuals of instruction for middle-class teenage girls.

A particularly successful example of the conduct-book genre was Hester Mulso Chapone's *Letters on the Improvement of the Mind, Addressed to a Young Lady*. First published in 1773, two years before Jane Austen's birth, by the end of the century it had been reprinted in individual editions at least sixteen times and was regularly bundled with other similar manuals to form small "Ladies' Libraries," as they were called, of improving texts. Chapone's book is addressed by an aunt to her niece in her "fifteenth year"[3]—the very age, of course, of Jane Austen as she writes the pieces assembled in *Volume the Second*. The coincidence is not accidental: not only does the teenage Austen mock the restrictive advice of such solemn works, but by announcing herself an authority "on the conduct of Young Women" she is turning the tables on the adult world, setting up the teenager as instructor. As a whole and in its parts, *Volume the Second* is best appreciated as a perverse conduct manual, a guide to behaving badly.

In content *Volume the Second* closely matches (and distorts) the educational syllabus proposed by works like Chapone's *Letters*, with their emphasis on rules for correct female behavior. Advice on a wide range of general issues, from reading, dress and desirable accomplishments to the control of moods and the demeanor expected of a daughter, wife, or mother (the only roles for which wellborn teenage girls were trained), was combined in conduct manuals of the time with more specific recommendations: to study botany, geology, history and especially chronology (tables of significant dates and events); to learn household management and the care of children; to avoid sentimental novels. Early in "Love and Freindship," the first story, Austen has a father observe: "Where . . . did you pick up this unmeaning Gibberish? You have been studying Novels I suspect" (p. 12). In terms of genre, these manuals fused devotional writings, marriage advice, recipe books and educational tracts. Their aim was to create on paper a composite character or model of the ideal young lady and to construct examples to guide her lifelong behavior in imagined situations. Accordingly, Chapone's *Letters* are divided into topics like "On the Regulation of the Heart and Affections" (letters 4 and 5); "On the Government of the Temper" (letter 6); "On Economy" (letter 7); "On the Manner and Course of Reading History" (letter 10).

It is no coincidence that the epistolary form dominates *Volume the Second*. Chapone's chapters are written as letters from aunt to niece, creating the illusion of an intimate conversational space open to the expression of opinions and moral debate. The novel written as a series of letters became popular in the late eighteenth century and grows out of the conduct manual. Epistolary novels tend to be dominated by the psychology and motives of the letter writer, and they openly invite interpretation as correspondents engage in reading one another's behavior and views directly off the page. In this sense, they close the distance between characters in fiction and their actual readers, since everyone is a reader. The first two works in *Volume the Second* are subtitled "novel in letters." Next comes "The History of England," described by its writer in anti-conduct-book fashion as "By a partial, prejudiced, & ignorant Historian" who has little patience with Chapone's championship of chronology; "N.B. There will be very few Dates in this History," declares the revisionist historian (p. 153). Its final sections again revert to letters: five letters that parody the dilemmas facing a young woman as she enters adult society are followed by the final "Scraps," three of which are also framed as letters.

In the conventional conduct book the letter is a vehicle for ideas; in the hands of the satirical author of *Volume the Second* it becomes a virtuoso performance by a series of exhibitionist egos who, possessing no social filters, quickly disclose themselves and squander any credibility. In this they are the very reverse of the ideal, which recommends scrutiny, discretion and regulation of the passions. It is as if the young Jane Austen has strategically animated and empowered a whole regiment of teenage girls to openly revolt, in their antisocial and extravagant behavior, against the conduct-book models of the schoolroom and the drawing room. Where the targets of *Volume the First* were diverse, *Volume the Second* displays a sustained focus.

The dedications reinforce this concentration; all but "Lesley Castle" (offered to her dashing undergraduate brother Henry) directly co-opt a female reader. "Love and Freindship" is dedicated to Austen's older cousin, the lively, fashionable and irreverent Eliza de Feuillide, who had married a Frenchman and was one of the most significant influences on her teenage years. Austen dedicates the schoolroom spoof "The History of England" to her sister Cassandra, in whose company she attended Mrs. La Tournelle's Ladies Boarding School in the Abbey House, Reading. Her cousin Jane Cooper, who shared an earlier period of schooling in Southampton with Jane and Cassandra and joined in Austen family theatricals at Christmas 1788–89, is the recipient of "A Collection of Letters," and the newborn Fanny Austen is given the benefit of her teenage aunt's "personal instruction" in "Scraps." Just as the epistolary form invokes— and parodies—a particular genre of teenage instruction, the dedications revisit Jane Austen's own educational formation and schooling and insinuate the reader as complicit with the revisionist writings that follow.

How do the young women in these stories behave? In "Love and Freindship" Laura wastes no time in ditching the polite exchange of voices usually implied by a series of letters: after the short opening note from her friend Isabel, the only point of view allowed to matter is her own; all the letters are written by Laura. Laura is resourceful, resilient and utterly self-serving. She lurches from one improbable adventure to another, bent solely on survival. Concern for others and the moderation of her own desires—qualities prized in the conventional young lady of sensibility of the conduct book—have become a distracting irrelevance; as she announces early on, "Tho' indeed my own misfortunes do not make less impression on me than they ever did, yet now I never feel for those of an other" (p. 6). Her partner in crime, Sophia, is equally self-interested; together they run amok, exposing the absurd inadequacy of conventional morality for the situations they encounter. They contract illegal marriages, abandon their husbands, steal from friends and relations and indulge in excessive—and insincere—emotional displays. No good little stay-at-home misses, they zigzag the length and breadth of Britain, from Wales to Middlesex and London and on to various locations in Scotland, breaking all the rules of proper female behavior and exploiting every opportunity for their own gain.

Charlotte Lutterell, one of the correspondents in "Lesley Castle," embodies a grotesque parody of the conduct manual's instructions on domestic management and household economy. When the sudden death of her sister's fiancé prevents their wedding, Charlotte's only concern is the food that will be wasted: "I had the mortification of finding that I had been Roasting, Broiling and Stewing both the Meat and Myself to no purpose" (p. 75). Food-fixated, Charlotte describes her sister's shock as leaving her face "as White as a Whipt syllabub." Toward the end of the volume bad behavior takes on a more extreme aspect: among the scraps addressed to little Fanny Austen is "A Letter from a Young Lady," in which the writer coolly confesses to every imaginable crime, including murdering her father and mother, and ends with the startling information that "I am now going to murder my Sister" (p. 247).

At the heart of the notebook, and in yet another swerve in direction, we discover two sisters who were also school friends sharing a joke about education. "The History of England" is illustrated with thirteen colored medallion portraits, each signed "C E Austen pinx[it]" ("Cassandra Elizabeth Austen painted [it]"). The only person to feature as a dedicatee in all three teenage notebooks, Cassandra, Austen's beloved sister, was her ideal reader, her most regular inspiration and, in her own right, as Jane lavishly recorded, "the finest comic writer of the present age."[4] Cassandra's cartoon portraits of kings and queens imitate those in Oliver Goldsmith's schoolroom classic, *The History of England*, and add a further interpretative dimension to the spoof "History," transforming it into a genuine collaboration.[5] Considerable care was evidently taken to allow sufficient space for the drawings as the pages were designed: on page 163, for instance, Austen begins a line of text and then erases it to make room for a portrait of Henry VIII. It has been suggested that some of Cassandra's portraits may also refer to members of the Austen family, with Jane standing in for her heroine Mary Queen of Scots, and her mother for the wicked Queen Elizabeth, who had Mary beheaded. (See the foot of page 171, where the two queens face each other in open antagonism.) Though the idea has attracted some controversy,[6] it is appealing and persuasive in the context of a parody conduct manual, at war with all proper authority, and a collection so thoroughly approving of rebellious children who, in the words of Laura in "Love and Freindship," have "so nobly disentangled themselves from the Shackles of Parental

Authority" (p. 26). It is worth noting that Austen's juvenilia in general take a satirical view of maternal behavior. Nor is this the most shocking aspect of the "History," in which Austen flirts dangerously, for the teenage daughter of a clergyman, with sexual innuendo, as in her allusion to James I's close friendships with young men (p. 181).

An unexpected aspect of *Volume the Second* is its Scottish flavor. In the opening story, Laura and Sophia find refuge in Macdonald-Hall, where their first act is to engineer the separation of Janetta and Graham, on the grounds that he is her father's choice (and therefore detestable) and—an equally serious charge—does not have "Auburn" hair. By the end, Laura has been united with an assortment of relations traveling together in the Edinburgh to Stirling coach, and we leave her a resident "in a romantic Village in the Highlands of Scotland" (p. 63). The next story, "Lesley Castle," is set in Perthshire, an area of Scotland much recommended for its picturesque scenery by late eighteenth-century travel writers. Here Matilda and Margaret Lesley are described by their young stepmother Susan Lesley as "two great, tall, out of the way, over-grown, Girls, just of a proper size to inhabit a Castle almost as Large in comparison as themselves" (p. 107). To their new mother's horror these "scotch Giants" "have no Music, but Scotch Airs, no Drawings but Scotch Mountains, and no books but Scotch Poems." She rounds off her criticisms with the declaration: "And I hate everything Scotch" (p. 109).

From red hair to mountains and folk songs, Jane Austen catalogues the latest craze for all things Scottish, relishing what she pokes fun at. The Scottish theme continues in her open allegiance—what she calls "my Attachment to the Scotch" (p. 184)—to the exiled (and now defunct) Stuart monarchy in her "prejudiced" "History of England." She had probably by now read Samuel Johnson and James Boswell's accounts of their 1773 travels in the Highlands, Sophia Lee's historical romance *The Recess* (1783–85), about the imagined daughters of Mary Queen of Scots, and perhaps even William Gilpin's most recent publication, *Observations, Relative Chiefly to Picturesque beauty . . . Particularly in the High-Lands of Scotland* (1789). She describes Gilpin, who was to remain one of her favorite writers, humorously in her "History" as among "those first of Men" (p. 168).

Samuel Johnson had gone to Scotland in the expectation of finding customs, people and scenery far stranger than the reality actually proved. His *Journey*, published in 1775, the year Jane Austen was born, registers this frustration in the curious angle of vision by which he teases things into an appearance of greater abnormality: his determination to find not only romance but "savage wildness" around every bend in the road, his curious emphasis on the size of the people.[7] Always an accomplished mimic, Austen catches his tone and exaggerates it further in Scottish riffs throughout *Volume the Second.* Her comic lists of Scottish names ("the M'Leods, The M'Kenzies, the M'Phersons"; p. 70) are also to be found in Johnson and Boswell, supplemented from the most famous Scottish play of all, Shakespeare's *Macbeth*, with a glance at Fanny Burney's melancholic Scotsman Mr. McCartney from her much admired *Evelina* (1778). At the same time, the motley collection of Scottish traits and facts paraded through *Volume the Second* can be read, like the inadequate grasp of geography that sets her characters on such idiosyncratic routes across Britain, as comment on the highly selective and inconsequential nature of female reading at the time.

Volume the Second, finished as she welcomed the birth of little Fanny Austen, marks the beginning of Jane Austen's lifelong celebration of the importance of aunts. "Now that you are become an Aunt, you are a person of some consequence & must excite great Interest whatever You do. I have always maintained the importance of Aunts as much as possible," wrote Jane to her niece Caroline Austen on October 30, 1815.[8] In *Mansfield Park* (1814) she would explore in Fanny Price, brought up by two bad aunts, the serious effects on adult prospects and happiness of an inadequate attention to female education. But in 1793 that would be some twenty years in the future. For now, Jane Austen glories in her newfound consequence as partial and prejudiced commentator on the proper reading for teenage girls.

This facsimile edition of *Volume the Second* has been produced with care to match the size of the original notebook, the appearance of its paper and the brown-black color of the iron gall ink that Jane Austen used. The transcription following the manuscript is that of the great twentieth-century Austen scholar Robert W. Chapman. Chapman was the first to edit Jane Austen's manuscripts in full and his early editions now have classic status.

NOTES

1. *Volume the Second* is held in the British Library, London, Add. MS. 59874. For more information on the physical appearance, history and ownership of this notebook, see the head note to *Volume the Second*, available at www.janeausten.ac.uk, the Digital Edition of Jane Austen's Fiction Manuscripts, ed. Kathryn Sutherland (2010).

2. Parenthetical page numbers refer to Jane Austen's own pagination of the notebook.

3. Hester Chapone, *Letters on the Improvement of the Mind, Addressed to a Young Lady*, 2nd ed., 2 vols. (London, 1773), vol. 1, p. 3.

4. *Jane Austen's Letters*, ed. Deirdre Le Faye, 3rd ed. (Oxford, England: Oxford University Press, 1995), p. 5, September 1, 1796.

5. For details of an Austen family copy of Oliver Goldsmith's *The History of England, from the Earliest Times to the Death of George II* (4 vols.; London, 1771), see David Gilson, "Jane Austen's Books," *The Book Collector* 23 (1974): pp. 44–62; and "Marginalia in Oliver Goldsmith's *The History of England*," in *Jane Austen, Juvenilia*, ed. Peter Sabor (Cambridge, England: Cambridge University Press, 2006), pp. 316–51. In the Austen copy, the engraved portraits of English monarchs in roundels at the chapter heads have been garishly colored in, according to family tradition, by the young Jane Austen.

6. See *Jane Austen's "The History of England" & Cassandra's Portraits*, ed. Annette Upfal and Christine Alexander (Sydney: Juvenilia Press, 2009), pp. xvii–xix: "The ultimate joke in the *History* is that the monarchs are represented by contemporary images of Austen family members and friends, including Jane Austen herself, and some of her siblings." Strong opposition has come from Deirdre Le Faye in the Jane Austen Society's *News Letter* 34 (March 2010): pp. 19–20.

7. See, for example, *Johnson's Journey to the Western Islands of Scotland and Boswell's Journal of A Tour to the Hebrides*, ed. R. W. Chapman (Oxford, England: Oxford University Press, 1970), pp. 37, 51, 59, 75. Johnson laments: "We came thither too late to see what we expected, a people of peculiar appearance, and a system of antiquated life."

8. *Jane Austen's Letters*, p. 294.

For my Brother Frank

iii   C. E. A.

For
my Brother Frank

C. E. A.

Ex dono mei Patris

Contents

Love and Freindship 1
Lesley-Castle ___ 67
The History of England . _ __ __ __ 153
Collection of Letters __ __ _____ 187
Scraps 237

To Madame La Comtesse De Feuillide

This Novel is inscribed

by

Her obliged Humble Servant

The Author

Love and Freindship

a novel

in a series of Letters –

Deceived in Freindship & Betrayed in Love

Letter the First

From Isabel to Laura

How often, in answer to my repeated
treaties that you would give my Daughter a
regular detail of the Misfortunes and Adventures
your Life, have you said "No, my freind never
ile I comply with your request till I may be
longer in Danger of again experiencing
~~such~~ *disadful* ones."

Surely that time is now at hand.
are this Day 55. If a woman may ever be
id to be in safety from the determined Perse-
rance of disagreable Lovers and the ~~~~ *cruel*
cutions of Obstinate Fathers, surely it mu
at such a time of Life.

Isabel.

tter 2

Laura to Isabel

Altho' I cannot agree with you in supposing

that I shall never again be exposed to Misfort

as unmerited as those I have already experien

yet to avoid the imputation of Obstinacy or

:nature, I will gratify the curiosity of you

Daughter; and may the fortitude with which

I have suffered the many afflictions of ~~that~~

past Life, prove to her a useful Lesson for th

support of those ~~which~~ which may befall her in

own.

Laura

Letter 3^d

Laura to Marianne

As the Daughter of my most in

:mate freind I think you entitled to that know

:ledge of my unhappy Story, which your Mo

has so often solicited me to give you.

My Father was a native of Ireland

& an inhabitant of Wales; my Mother was th

tural Daughter of a Scotch Peer by an italian
opera girl — I was born in Spain & received
my Education at a Convent in France.

When I had reached my eighteenth
Year I was recalled by my Parents to my pater=
nal roof in Wales. Our mansion was situated
in one of the most romantic parts of the Vale
of Uske. Tho' my Charms are now considerably
softened and somewhat impaired by the Misfor=
tunes I have undergone, I was once beautiful.
But lovely as I was the graces of my Person were
the least of my Perfections. Of every accom=
plishment accustomary to my sex, I was
Mistress. — When in the Convent, my progress
had always exceeded my instructions, my
                    had been
Acquirements were wonderfull for my age,
      had
and I shortly surpassed my Masters.

In my mind, every Virtue that could
on
adorn was centered; it was the Rendez=vous
of every good Quality & the place of appiness

6 of every noble sentiment.

A sensibility too tremblingly alive to every affliction of my Freinds, my acquaint. and particularly to every affliction of my own was my only fault, if a fault it could be ca

Alas! how altered now! Tho' indeed my misfortunes do not make less impression one than they ever did, yet now I never feel for those of another. — My accomplishment too, begin to fade — I can neither sing so we nor Dance so gracefully as I once did — and have entirely forgot the Minuet Dela Cour —

Adeiu.

Laura

Letter 4th

Laura to Marianne

Our neighbourhood was small, for it consiste only of your Mother. She may probably have alre told you that being left by her Parents in indigen Circumstances she had retired into Wales on econ

l motives. There it was, our friendship first
menced—. Isabel was then one and twenty—
o' pleasing both in her Person and Manners
(ween ourselves) she never possessed the hun-
redth part of my Beauty or Accomplishments.
Isabel had seen the World. She had passed 2
ars at one of the first Boarding-schools in
ndon; had spent a fortnight in Bath & had
upped
pt one night in Southampton.

"Beware my Laura (she would often say)
ware of the insipid Vanities and idle Dissipation
the Metropolis of England; Beware of the
meaning Luxuries of Bath & of the stink:
fish of Southampton."

"Alas! (exclaimed I) how am I to avoid
se evils I shall never be exposed to? What
babilitz is there of my ever tasting the dissipation
London, the Luxuries of Bath, or the stinking
ils of Southampton? I who am doomed to
ste my Days of Youth & Beauty in an

humble Cottage in the Vale of Uske."

Ah! little did I then think I was ordain
so soon to quit that humble Cottage for the
deceitfull Pleasures of the World.

adieu

Laura —

Letter 5th

Laura to Marianne

One Evening in December as my Father
my Mother and myself, were arranged in so
:al converse round our Fireside, we were on a
sudden, greatly astonished, ~~considerably a~~
~~mazed and somewhat surprized~~, by hearing a
violent knocking on the outward Door of our
rustic Cot.

My Father started — "What noise is th
(said he) "It sounds like a loud rapping at on
Door" — (replied my Mother) "it does indeed."(cried
"I am of your opinion; (said my Father) it cer

does appear to proceed from some uncommon
~~violence~~ excited against our unoffending Door."
"Yes (exclaimed I) I cannot help thinking it
must be somebody who knocks for admittance."

"That is another point (replied he;) ~~We can~~
~~pretend to assert that any one knocks, that~~
~~must not pretend to determine on what may~~
~~may not pass. I can I rather imagine that~~
the person may Knock — tho' that some
~~knock at the Door that somebody does. Yet~~
~~he does, rap at the Door, I am partly convinced~~
~~we have no ocular dem——~~ *.*

Here, a 2d tremendous rap interrupted
my Father in his speech and somewhat alarmed
my Mother and me.

"Had we not better go and see who it is?
(said she) the Servants are out." "I think we had."
(replied I.) "Certainly, (added my Father) by all
means." "Shall we go now?" (said my Mother.)
"The sooner the better." (answered he.) "Oh! let ~~no~~
~~time be lost.~~ ~~immediately~~." (cried I.)

A third more violent Rap than ever
again assaulted our ears. "I am certain there is

somebody knocking at the Door." (said my Moth.
"I think there must," (replied my Father) "I
fancy the servants are returned; (said I) I thin
I hear Mary going to the Door." "I'm glad of it.
(cried my Father) for I long to know who it is

I was right in my Conjecture; for Mary
instantly entering the Room, informed us that
young Gentleman & his Servant were at the
Door, who had lossed their way, were very cold
and begged leave to warm themselves by our
fire. "Wont you admit them?" (said I) "You have
no objection, my Dear?" (said my Father.) "No
in the World" (replied my Mother.)

Mary, without waiting for any further
commands immediately left the room and
quickly returned introducing the most beautiful
and amieable Youth, I had ever beheld. The
servant, she kept to herself.

My natural Sensibility had already

greatly affected by the sufferings of the unfortunate
stranger and no sooner did I first behold him, than
~~that on him the happiness or Misery of my~~
felt ~~xxxxxxxxxxxxxxxxxxxxxxxxxxxxxxx~~
future Life must depend. — adieu

            Laura

Letter 6th

     Laura to Marianne

       The noble Youth informed us that his
name was Lindsay — for particular reasons how:
ever I shall conceal it under that of Talbot.
He told us that he was the son of an English
Baronet, that his Mother had been many years
more and that he had a Sister of the middle
size. "My Father (he continued) is a mean and
mercenary wretch — it is only to such particular
friends as this Dear Party that I would thus
betray his failings. Your Virtues my amiable
Polydore (addressing himself to my father) yours
dear Claudia and yours my Charming Laura
call on me to repose in you my Confidence".

We bowed. "My Father, seduced by the false glare of Fortune and the Deluding Pomp of Title, insisted on my giving my hand to Lady Dorothea. No never exclaimed I. Lady Dorothea is lovely and Engaging; I prefer no woman to her; but Know Sir, that I scorn to marry her in compliance with your Wishes. ~~if you wish I should~~. No! Never shall it be said that I obliged my Father."

We all admired the noble Manliness of his reply. He continued.

"Sir Edward was surprized; he had perhaps little expected to ~~know not~~ meet with so spirited an opposition to his Will. "Where Edward in the name of wonder (said he) did you pick up this unmeaning Gibberish? You have been studying novels I suspect." I scorned to answer: it would have been beneath my Dignity. I mounted my Horse and followed by my faithful William set forwards for my Aunts."

"My Father's house is situated in B

...rdshire, my Aunts in Middlesex, and tho' I flatter myself with being a tolerable proficient in Geography, I know not how it happened, but I found myself entering this beautifull Vale which I find is in South Wales, when I had expected to have reached my Aunts."

"After having wandered some time on the Banks of the Uske without knowing which way to go, I began to lament my cruel Destiny in the bitterest and most pathetic Manner. It was now perfectly dark, not a single Star was there to direct my steps, and I know not what might have befallen me, had I not at length discerned thro' the solemn Gloom that surrounded me a distant Light, which as I approached I discovered to be the chearfull Blaze of a fire. Impelled by the combination of Misfortunes under which I laboured, namely Fear, Cold and Hunger I hesitated not to

ask admittance which at length I have g
:ed; and now my adorable Laura (continued
he taking my Hand) when may I hope to re
:ceive that reward of all the painfull suf
:ferings I have undergone during the cours
of my attachment to you, to which I have
aspired? Oh! when will you reward me
with yourself?"

"This instant, Dear and amiable Edwar
(replied I.) We were immediately united by
my Father, who tho' he had never taken o
:ders had been bred to the Church.

adieu

Laura.

Letter 7th
Laura to Marianne

We remained but a few Days after
our Marriage, in the Vale of Uske — After
taking an affecting Farewell of my Father

Mother and my Isabel, I accompanied
ward to his aunt's in Middlesex. Philippa
eived us both with every expression of
ectionate Love. My arrival was indeed
most agreable surprize to her as she had
t only been totally ignorant of my marriage
th her Nephew, but had never even had the ~~not~~ ~~the~~
ightest idea of there being such a person in the
ld.

Augusta, the sister of Edward was on
isit to her when we arrived. ~~Her~~ I found
exactly what her Brother had described
to be — of the middle size. She received
with equal surprize though not with
al Cordiality, as Philippa. There was a
isagreable Coldness and forbidding Reserve
her reception of me which was equally
istressing and Unexpected. None of that
teresting Sensibility or amiable Sympathy

in her Manners and Address to me when we
first met which should have distinguished
our introduction to each other—. Her Language
was neither warm, nor affectionate, her expres
:ons of regard were neither animated nor co
:dial; her arms were not opened to receive
me to her Heart, tho' my own were extended
to press her to mine.

A short Conversation between Augus
and her Brother; which I accidentally overh
increased my Dislike to her, and convinced me
that her Heart was no more formed for the
soft ties of Love than for the endearing in
:tercourse of Friendship.

"But do you think that my Fat
will ever be reconciled to this imprudent con
:tion?" (said Augusta.)

"Augusta (replied the noble Youth) I
thought you had a better opinion of me, th

imagine I would so abjectly degrade myself
as to consider my Father's Concurrence in any
of my Affairs, either of Consequence or concern
me —. Tell me Augusta tell me with sin:
cerity; did you ever know me consult his
Inclinations or follow his Advice in the least
trifling Particular since the age of fifteen?"

"Edward (replied she) you are surely too
diffident in your own praise —. Since you
were fifteen only! — My dear Brother since
you were five years old, I entirely acquit
you of having ever willingly contributed to the
satisfaction of your Father. But still I am
not without apprehensions of your being
shortly obliged to degrade yourself in your
own eyes by seeking a support for your Wife
in the Generosity of Sir Edward."

"Never, never Augusta will I so demean

(said Edward)

myself. Support! What support will Laura

want which she can receive from him?"

"Only those very insignificant ones of

Victuals and Drink." (answered she.)

"Victuals and Drink! (replied my Husband

in a most nobly contemptuous Manner) and

dost thou then imagine that there is no other

support for an exalted Mind (such as is my

Laura's) than the mean and indelicate em-

ployment of Eating and Drinking?"

"None that I know of, so efficacious
returned
(replied Augusta)

"And did you then never feel the

pleasing Pangs of Love, Augusta? (replied my
                   Does
Edward). Did it appear impossible to your
           corrupted
vile and Vulgar Palate, to exist on Love? Could

you not conceive the Luxury of living in

every Distress that Poverty can inflict, with

object of your tenderest affection?"

"You are too ridiculous (said Augusta) to
argue with; perhaps however you may in
time be convinced that " ....

Here I was prevented ~~interrupted~~ from hearing the
remainder of her speech, by the appearance of
a very Handsome young Woman, who was
ushered into the Room at the Door of which I
had been listening. On hearing her announce
the Name of "Lady Dorothea", I instantly
quitted my Post and followed her into the
Parlour, for I well remembered that she was
the Lady, proposed as a Wife for my Edward by
the Cruel and Unrelenting Baronet.

Altho' Lady Dorothea's visit was nomi-
=nally to Philippa and Augusta, yet I have
some reason to imagine that (acquainted with
the Marriage and arrival of Edward) to see me

was a principal motive to it.

I soon perceived that tho' Lovely a
Elegant in her Person and tho' Easy and [?]
in her Address, she was of that inferior or[der]
of Beings with regard to Delicate Feeling, te[nder]
Sentiments, and refined Sensibility, of which
Augusta was once.

She staid but half an hour and [?]
ther in the Course of her Visit, confided to [me]
any of her Secret thoughts, nor requested me [to]
confide in her, any of Mine. You will eas[ily]
imagine therefore my Dear Marianne tha[t]
I could not feel any ardent affection or ve[ry]
sincere Attachment for Lady Dorothea.

Adieu

Laura.

Letter 8th Laura to Marianne, in continuation

Lady Dorothea had not left us long

fore another visitor as unexpected a one as her
Lyship, was announced. It was Sir Edward,
who informed by Augusta of her Brother's marriage, came doubtless to reproach him for
having dared to unite himself to me without
his Knowledge. But Edward foreseeing his
design, approached him with heroic fortitude
as soon as he entered the Room, and addressed
him in the following Manner.

"Sir Edward, I know the motive of
your Journey here — You come with the
base Design of reproaching me for having
entered into an indissoluble engagement
with my Laura without your Consent.
But Sir, I glory in the Act — It is my
greatest boast that I have incurred the
displeasure of my Father!"

So saying, he took my hand and whilst
Sir Edward, Philippa, and Augusta were
doubtless reflecting

with admiration on his undaunted Brav

led me from the Parlour to his Father's Car

which yet remained at the Door and in wh

we were instantly conveyed from the pu

of Sir Edward.

The Postilions had at first receiv

orders only to take the London road; as so

as we had sufficiently reflected However, u

ordered them to Drive to M—. the seat of Edw

most particular freind, which was but a few mile

distant.

                  a few hours

At M—. we arrived in ~~less than an~~

~~hour;~~ and on sending in our names were

immediately admitted to Sophia, the wife

Edward's freind. After having been depriv

during the course of 3 weeks of a real freind

such I term your Mother) imagine my tra

sports at beholding one, most truly worth

of the Name. Sophia was rather above the m

ize; most elegantly formed. A soft languor
spread over her lovely features, but increased
their Beauty —. It was the Characteristic
of her Mind —. She was all sensibility and
feeling. We flew into each others arms &
after having exchanged vows of mutual
Freindship for the rest of our Lives, instantly
unfolded to each other the most inward
Secrets of our Hearts —. We were interrupted
in this Delightfull Employment by the
Entrance of Augustus, (Edward's freind) who
was just returned from a solitary ramble.

Never did I see such an affecting Scene
as was the meeting of Edward & Augustus.
"My Life! my Soul!" (exclaimed the former)
"My adorable angel!" (replied the latter) as
they flew into each other's arms. — It was too
pathetic for the feelings of Sophia and
myself — We fainted Alternately on a Sofa.

                                    adieu
                                    Laura

Letter the 9th – From the same to the same

~~When we were somewhat recovered from the~~
~~overpowering effusion of~~

Towards the close of the Day we received
the following Letter from Philippa.

"Sir Edward is greatly incensed by your abrupt
departure; he has taken back Augusta with him
to Bedfordshire. Much as I wish to enjoy again your
charming society, ~~yet~~ I cannot determine to
snatch you from that, of such dear & deserving
friends – When your Visit to them is terminated,
I trust you will return to the arms of your
                                    "Philippa"

We returned a suitable answer to this affectionate
Note & after thanking her for her kind invitation
assured her that we would certainly avail ourselves
of it, whenever we might have no other place to go to.
Tho' certainly nothing could to any reasonable Being
have appeared more satisfactory, than so grateful
a reply to her invitation, yet I know not how it was,
but she was certainly capricious enough to be displeased
with our behaviour and in a few weeks after, either
to revenge our Conduct, or relieve her own solitude, ma-

young and illiterate Fortune-hunter. This imprudency
(tho' we were sensible that it would probably
prive us of that fortune which Philippa had ever taught
to expect) could not on our own accounts, excite
in our exalted Minds a single sigh; yet fearfull
it might prove a source of endless misery
the deluded Bride—our trembling sensibility was
ably affected when we were first informed of the
ent. The affectionate Entreaties of Augustus and
hia that we would for ever consider their House
ur Home, easily prevailed on us to determine never
to leave them—. In the society of my Edward &
is amiable Pair, I passed the happiest moments
my Life; our time was most delightfully spent,
mutual Protestations of Freindship, & in vows
unalterable Love, in which we were secure
in being interrupted, by intruding & disagreable
itors, as Augustus & Sophia had on their first
rance in the Neighbourhood, taken due care to
orm the surrounding Families, that as their
ppiness centered wholly in themselves, they
hed for no other society. But alas! my dear
rianne such Happiness as I enjoyed their was too

perfect to be lasting. a most severe & unex=
=ed Blow at once destroyed every Sensation of
Pleasure. Convinced as you must be from w
I have already told you concerning Augustus ?
Sophia, that there never were ~~were~~ a happier Cou
I need not I imagine inform you that their unio
had been contrary to the inclinations of th
Cruel & Mercenery Parents; who had vainly e
=deavoured with obstinate Perseverance to fo
them into a Marriage with those whom they had
abhorred; but with an Heroic Fortitude worth
to be related & admired, they had both constan
refused to submit to such ~~xxxx~~ despotic ~~xxxxxx~~ Po

After having so nobly disentangled th
=selves from the Shackles of Parental aut
=rity, by a Clandestine Marriage, they were de
=mined never to forfeit the good opinion they ha
gained in the World, in so doing, by accepting
any proposals of reconciliation that migh
offered them by their Fathers — to this farth
tryal of their noble independance however
never were exposed.

They had been married but a few month

hen our visit to them commenced during which
e they had been amply supported by a conside:
ble sum of money which Augustus had gracefully
loined from his Unworthy Father's Escritoire, a
 days before his union with Sophia.

By our arrival their Expenses were con:
iderably encreased tho' their means for supplying
m were then nearly exhausted. But they, Exalted
atures! scorned to reflect a moment on their pe:
niary Distresses & would have blushed at the
a of paying their Debts. — Alas! what was their
ward for such disinterested Behaviour! The beau:
ull Augustus was arrested and we were all un:
ue. Such perfidious Treachery in the merciless
petrators of the Deed will shock your gentle na:
e Dearest Marianne as much as it then affected
Delicate Sensibility of ~~Augus~~ Edward, Sophia,
r Laura, & of Augustus himself. To compleat
h unparalleled Barbarity we were informed that
Execution in the House would shortly take place.
! what could we do but what we did! We
hed & fainted on the Sofa. Adieu

Laura

Letter 10th. Laura in continuation

When we were somewhat recovered fro
the overpowering Effusions of our Grief, Edwar
desired that we would consider what was the s
prudent step to be taken in our unhappy situat
while he repaired to his imprisoned friend to la
:ment over his misfortunes. We promised tha
we
he would, & he set forwards on his Journey to Tou
During his absence we faithfully complied wi
his Desire & after the most mature Deliberation, a
length agreed that the best thing we could d
was to leave the House; of which we every mom
expected the Officers of Justice to take popession.
We waited therefore with the greatest impatie
for the return of Edward in order to impart
him the result of our Deliberations —. But no
:ward appeared — In vain did we count the tedio
Moments of his absence — in vain did we weep
in vain even did we sigh — no Edward returned —
This was too cruel, too unexpected a Blow to ou
Gentle Sensibility — we could not support it — we
could only faint —. At length collecting all the Re
:lution I was Mistress of, I arose & after packing
some necessary apparel for Sophia & myself, I a

d her to a Carriage I had ordered & we instantly
out for London. As the Habitation of Augustus
within twelve miles of Town, it was not long
we arrived there, & no sooner had we entered
the Town than letting down one of the Front Glasses
quired of every decent-looking Person that we
ed "If they had seen my Edward"?

But as we drove too rapidly to allow them
answer my repeated Enquiries, I gained little, or
eed, no information concerning him. "Where am I
rive?" said the Postilion. "To Newgate Gentle
M (replied I), to see Augustus." "Oh! no, no, (ex:
imed Sophia) I cannot go to Newgate; I shall not
able to support the sight of my Augustus in so
el a confinement – my feelings are sufficiently
cked by the recital, of his Distress, but to behold
wile overpower my sensibility." As I perfectly
ed with her in the Justice of her Sentiments
Postilion was instantly directed to return into
Country. You may perhaps have been somewhat
rized my Dearest Marianne, that in the Dis:
s I then endured, destitute of any Support,
vided with any Habitation, I should never once

have remembered my Father & Mother or my pater
Cottage in the Vale of Uske. To account for this seeming
forgetfulness I must inform you of a trifling circum
:stance concerning them which I have as yet never
mentioned — The death of my Parents a few weeks a
my Departure, is the circumstance I allude to. By
their decease I became the lawfull Inheritress of their
House & Fortune. But alas! the House had never been
their own & their Fortune had only been an Annuity
on their own Lives. — Such is the Depravity of the Wor
To your Mother I should have returned with Pleasure
should have been happy to have introduced to her
my Charming Sophia & should with Chearfullness ha
passed the remainder of my Life in their dear Societ
in the Vale of Uske, had not one Obstacle to the
execution of so agreable a Scheme, intervened; w
was the Marriage & Removal of your Mother to a
Distant part of Ireland. Adieu.

     Laura.

Letter 11th
   Laura in continuation —

   "I have a Relation in Scotland (said Sophia to
as we left London) who I am certain would not hesitat

receiving me: "Shall I order the Boy to drive there?"
d I- but instantly recollecting myself, exclaimed, "Alas
or it will be too long a Journey for the Horses." Un:
illing however to act only from my own inadequate
owledge of the Strength & Abilities of Horses, I consulted
Postilion, who was entirely of my Opinion concerning
affair. We therefore determined to change Horses
the next Town & to travel Post the remainder of
Journey: - . When we arrived at the last Inn we
e to stop at, which was but a few miles from the
se of Sophia's Relation, unwilling to intrude our
ity on them unexpected & unthought of, we wrote a
elegant & well penned Note to him containing an
unt of our Destitute & melancholy Situation, and of
intention to spend some months with him in Scot:
d. As soon as we had dispatched this Letter, we
ediately prepared to follow ~~him~~ it in person & were
mping into the Carriage for that Purpose when our
ntion was attracted by the Entrance of a coronetted
h & 4 into the Inn-yard. A Gentleman considerably
anced in years, descended from it - . At his first
earance my sensibility was wonderfully affected
er I had gazed at him a 2d time, an instinctive
pathy whispered to my Heart, that he was my

Grandfather.

Convinced that I could not be mistaken in
conjecture I instantly sprang from the Carriage
had just entered, & following the Venerable Stran
into the Room he had been shewn to, I threw my
on my knees before him & besought him to acknow
me as his Grand Child. — He started, & after hav
attentively examined my features, raised me fro
the Ground & throwing his Grand-fatherly arms ar
my Neck, exclaimed, "Acknowledge thee! Yes dear
:semblance of my Laurina & my Laurina's Daugh
sweet image of my Claudia & my Claudia's moth
I do acknowledge thee as the Daughter of the one
& the Grandaughter of the other." While he was th
tenderly embraceing me, Sophia astonished at my
precipitate Departure, entered the Room in sear
of me .. no sooner had she caught the eye of
venerable Peer, than he exclaimed with ev'ry m
of Astonishment — "Another Grandaughter! Yes y
I see you are the Daughter of my Laurina's eld
Girl; your resemblance to the beauteous Matil
sufficiently proclaims it. "Oh! replied Sophia, when
first beheld you the instinct of Nature whispe
me that we were in some degree related — But
whether Grandfathers, or Grandmothers, I could

tend to determine." He folded her in his arms, and
lst they were tenderly embracing, the Door of the
tment opened and a most beautifull young man
eared. On perceiving him Lord St Clair started &
ating back a few paces, with uplifted Hands, said,
other Grand-child! what an unexpected Happeness
his! to discover in the space of 3 minutes, as
ny of my Descendants! This, I am certain is Phi-
nder the son of my Laurina's 3d Girl the amiable
tha; there wants now but the presence of Gustavus
mpleat the Union of my Laurina's Grand children."
"And here he is; (said a gracefull Youth who that
ant entered the room) here is the Gustavus you de:
to see. I am the son of Agatha your Laurina's 4th
ungest Daughter." "I see you are indeed; replied Lord
air — But tell me (continued he looking fearfully
rds the Door) tell me, have I any other Grand-
dren in the House." "None my Lord." "Then I will
ide for you ale without farther delay — Here are
nknotes of 50£ each — Take them & remember
ve done the Duty of a Grandfather —." He instantly
the Room & immediately afterwards the House.
                    Adeiu.

                        Laura.

Letter the 12th

Laura in continuation

You may imagine how greatly we were surpris
by the sudden departure of Lord St Clair. "Ignoble
-vire!" exclaimed Sophia. "Unworthy Grandfather!" sai
instantly fainted in each other's arms. How long we re
:ed in this situation I know not; but when we recove
we found ourselves alone, without either Gustavus, 'E
:lander, or the Bank-notes. As we were deploring
our unhappy fate, the Door of the Apartment open
& "Macdonald" was announced. He was Sophia's
:sin. The haste with which he came to our releif s
soon after the receipt of our Note, spoke so greatly in
favour that I hesitated not to pronounce him at
first sight, a tender & sympathetic Freind. Alas!
little deserved the name — for though he told us
that he was much concerned at our Misfortunes, y
by his own account it appeared that the perus
of them, had neither drawn from him a single
nor induced him to bestow one curse on our vind
:tive Stars. — He told Sophia that his Daughter
depended on her returning with him to Macdon
— Hall; & that as his Cousin's freind he should be
happy to see me there also. To Macdonald-Hall,

we went, and were received with great kindness,
Janetta the daughter of Macdonald, & the Mistress of the
sion. Janetta was then only fifteen; naturally
disposed, endowed with a susceptible Heart, and a
pathetic Disposition, she might, had these amiable
lities been properly encouraged, have been an orna:
nt to human Nature; but unfortunately her
ther possessed not a soul sufficiently exalted to ad:
ie so promising a Disposition, and had endeavoured
very means in his power to prevent its encreasing
her Years. He had actually so far extinguished the
ral noble Sensibility of her Heart, as to prevail on her
cept an offer from a young Man of his Recommen:
tion. They were to be married in a few Months, and
ham, was in the House when we arrived. We soon
through his Character—. He was just such a Man
re might have expected to be the choice of Macdonald.
said he was sensible, well-informed, and agreable;
did not pretend to Judge of such trifles, but as we
convinced he had no soul, that he had never read
Sorrows of Werter, & that his Hair bore not the
t resemblance to auburn, we were certain that
etta could feel no affection for him; or at least

that she ought to feel none. The very circumstance
his being her father's choice too, was so much in his
disfavour, that had he been deserving her, in every
respect yet that of itself ought to have been a suffi
:ent reason in the Eyes of Fanetta for rejecting him.
These considerations we were determined to repres
to her in their proper light & doubted not of meeti
with the desired Success from one naturally so w
disposed; whose errors in the affair had only ari
from a want of proper confidence in her own
:nion, & a suitable contempt of her father's. We
found her indeed all that our warmest wishe
could have hoped for; we had no difficulty to con
:vince her that it was impossible she could lov
Graham, or that it was her Duty to disobey he
Father; the only thing at which she rather seem
to hesitate was our assertion that she must be
attached to some other Person. For some time, sh
persevered in declaring that she knew no other
young Man for whom she had the smallest Affec
but upon explaining the impossibility of such a s
she said that she believed she did like Captain M.

:ze

...er than any one she knew besides. This confession
...isfied us and after having enumerated the good
...lities of Mr Kenzie & assured her ^that she was violently
...ove with him, we desired to know whether he
...ever in anywise declared his affection to her.
...far from having ever declared it, I have no rea:
...to imagine ^that he has ever felt any for me." said
...tia. "That he certainly adores you (replied Sophia)
...can be no doubt _. The Attachment must be
...iprocal _. Did he never gaze on you with admiration
...derly press your hand _ drop an involuntary
...& leave the room abruptly?" "Never (replied she)
...I remember _ he has always left the room indeed
...n his visit has been ended, but has never gone
...particularly abruptly or without making a bow."
...deed my Love (said I) you must be mistaken _
...it is absolutely impossible that he should ever
...left you but with ~~with~~, Confusion, Despair
...ecipitation _. Consider but for a moment Janetta
...u must be convinced how absurd it is to sup:
...se that he could ever make a bow, or behave
...~~like other People~~. any other Person."
Having settled this Point to

our, satisfaction, the next we took into consideration
was, to determine in what manner we should in:
:form Mc Kenzie of the favourable Opinion Janetta
entertained of him... We at length agreed to acquaint
him with it by an anonymous Letter which Sophy
drew up in the following Manner.

"Oh! happy Lover of the beautifull Janetta,
Oh! enviable Possessor of _her_ Heart whose hand is
destined to another, why do you thus delay a con:
:fession of your attachment to the amiable Object
of it? Oh! consider that a few weeks will at once
put an end to every flattering Hope that you now
now entertain, by uniting the unfortunate Victim
of her father's Cruelty to the execrable & detested
Graham."

"Alas! why do you thus so cruelly connive
at the projected Misery of her & of yourself by delaying
to communicate that scheme which has doubtless
long possessed your imagination? A secret Union
will at once secure the felicity of both."

The amiable Mc Kenzie, whose modesty as he
afterwards assured us had been the only reason of
his having so long concealed the violence of his

tion for Janetta, on receiving this Billet flew on
wings of Love to Macdonald Hall, and so power:
ey pleaded his Attachment to her who inspired
that after a few more private interveiws, So:
ia & I experienced the satisfaction of seeing
m depart for Gretna-Green, which they chose
the celebration of their Nuptials, in preference
~~prrvit wonderful billity~~, although
any other place ~~a sit end a matt agreeable~~
~~s~~ a considerable distance
~~in~~ from Macdonald Hall. Adeiu —

     Laura —

ter the 13th

   Laura in Continuation

  They had been gone nearly a couple of Hours, before
er Macdonald or Graham had entertained any
icion of the affair. And they might not even
have suspected it, ~~had it not~~ but for the fol:
ing little Accident. Sophia happening one Day to
a private Drawer in Macdonald's Library, with
of her own keys, discovered that it was the
e where he kept his Papers of consequence
amongst
~~the~~ them some bank notes of considerable
ount. This discovery she imparted to me; and
ing agreed together that it would be a proper
ment of so vile a Wretch as Macdonald to

deprive him of money, perhaps dishonestly gain
it was determined that the next time we sho
either of us happen to go that way, we would
one or more of the Bank notes from the drawer. ?
well meant Plan we had often successfully put a
Execution; but alas! on the very day of Ianetta's Ep
as Sophia was majestically removing the 5.th Ban
-note from the Drawer to her own purse, she wa
suddenly most impertinently interrupted in he
employment by the entrance of Macdonald hims
in a most abrupt & precipitate Manner. Sophe
(who though naturally all winning sweetness co
when occascions demanded it call forth the Digas
of her sex) instantly put on a most forbiding loo
& darting an angry frown on the undaunted cu
:prit, demanded in a haughty tone of voice "whe
:fore her retirement was thus insolently broke
in on.3" The unblushing Macdonald, without eu
endeavouring to exculpate himself from the cr
he was charged with, meanly endeavoured to
:proach Sophia with ignobly defrauding him
his Money... The dignity of Sophia was wound

etch (exclaimed she, hastily replacing the Bank-
te in the Drawer) how darest thou to accuse
of an act, of which the bare idea makes me
oh?" The base wretch was still unconvinced &
inued to upbraid the justly-offended Sophia in
h opprobrious Language, that at length he so greatly
oked the gentle sweetness of her Nature, as to
uce her to revenge herself on him by informing
n of Janetta's Elopement, and of the active Part
had both taken in the affair. At this period
heir Quarrel I entered the Library and was as
may imagine equally offended as Sophia at the
grounded Accusations of the malevolent and con-
mptible Macdonald. "Base Miscreant! (cried I)
canst thou thus undauntedly endeavour to sully
spotless reputation of such bright Excellence? Why
t thou not suspect my innocence as soon?"
"Be satisfied Madam (replied he) I do suspect it,
refore must desire that you will both leave this
se in less than half an hour."
"We shall go willingly; (answered Sophia) our

hearts have long detested thee, & nothing but our
freindship for My Daughter could have induced
us to remain so long beneath thy roof."

"Your Freindship for my Daughter has indeed
been most powerfully exerted by throwing her
into the arms of an unprincipled Fortune-hun
(replied he)

"Yes, (exclaimed I) amidst every misfortune,
will afford us some consolation to reflect that
by this one act of Freindship to Janetta, we have
amply discharged every Obligation that we have
received from her father."

"It must indeed be a most gratefull reflection
to your exalted minds." (said he.)

As soon as we had packed up our war
-robe & valuables, we left Macdonald Hall, & after
having walked about a mile & a half we sate
down by the side of a clear limpid stream to
refresh our exhausted limbs. The place was su
:ed to meditation —. A Grove of full-grown Elms she
:tered us from the East —. A Bed of full-grown Nettle
from the West —. Before us ran the murmuring br
& behind us ran the turn-pike road. We were in
a mood for contemplation & in a Disposition to enj

beautifull a spot. A mutual silence which had
some time reigned between us, was at length
[brok]e by my exclaiming – "What a lovely Scene! Alas
[why] are not Edward & augustus here to enjoy its
[Bea]uties with us?"

"Ah! my beloved Laura (cried Sophia) for pity's
[sak]e forbear recalling to my remembrance the
[un]happy situation of my imprisoned Husband. Alas,
[wha]t would I not give to learn the fate of my augus:
[tu]s! – to know if he is still in Newgate, or if he
[is] yet hung. – But never shall I be able so far to
[con]quer my tender sensibility as to enquire after
[him]. Oh! do not I beseech you ever let me again
[hea]r you repeat his beloved Name –. It affects me
[too] deeply –. I cannot bear to hear him mentioned
[it] wounds my feelings."

"Excuse me my Sophia for having thus un:
[wil]lingly offended you –" replied I – and then chang:
[ing] the conversation, desired her to admire the
[nob]le Grandeur of the Elms which Sheltered us
[from] the Eastern Zephyr. "Alas! my Laura (returned
[she]) avoid so melancholy a subject, I intreat you –
Do not again wound my Sensibility by Observa:
:tions

on those elms –. They remind me of augustus –. He was like them, tall, magestic – he possessed that noble grandeur which you admire in them."

I was silent, fearfull lest I might any more unwillingly distress her by fixing on another subject of conversation which might again remind her of Augustus.

"Why do you not speak my Laura? (said she after a short pause) I cannot support this silence – you must not leave me to my own reflections; they ever recur to Augustus."

"What a beautifull Sky! (said I) How charming is the azure varied by those delicate streaks of white!"

"Oh! my Laura (replied she hastily withdrawing her Eyes from a momentary glance at the sky) do not thus distress me by calling my attention to an object which so cruelly reminds me of my Augustus's blue sattin waistcoat striped with white! In pity to your unhappy friend avoid a subject so distressing." What I do? The feelings of Sophia were at that time so exquisite, & the tenderness she felt for Augustus so poignant that I had not power to start any o

...ie, piety fearing that it might in some unforseen
...anner again awaken all her sensibility by directing
...thoughts to her Husband. — Yet to be silent
...ld be cruel, she had intreated me to talk.
From this Dilemma I was most fortunately
...ived by an accident truly apropos; it was the
...ky overturning of a Gentleman's Phaeton, on
...road which ran murmuring behind us. It
...s a most fortunate accident as it diverted the
...ention of Sophia from the melancholy reflections
...anguish which she had been before indulging.
...e instantly quitted our seats & ran to the rescue
...those who but afew moments before had been
...so elevated a situation as a fashionably high
...haeton, but who were now laid low and sprawling
...the Dust... "What an ample subject for reflection
...the uncertain Enjoyments of this World, would
...that Phaeton & the life of Cardinal Wolsey afford
..."inking Mind"/ said I to Sophia as we were
...stening to the field of action.
....She had not time to answer me, for every
...ght was now engaged by the horrid Spectacle
...e us. Two gentlemen most elegantly attired

but weltering in their blood was what first struck
Eyes — we approached — they were Edward & Augustus
Yes dearest Marianne they were our Husbands
Sophia shrieked & fainted on the Ground — I scream
& instantly ran mad —. We remained thus mut
:ally deprived of our Senses, some minutes, & on r
:gaining them were deprived of them again —. For
an Hour & a Quarter did we continue in this u
:fortunate Situation — Sophia fainting every mo
:ment & I running Mad as often —. At length
Groan from the hapless Edward (who alone retaine
any share of Life) restored us to ourselves —. Had
indeed before imagined that either of them live
we should have been more sparing of our Greif —
as we had supposed when we first beheld them
that they were no more, we knew that noth
could remain to be done but what we were
about —. No sooner therefore did we hear my
Edward's groan than postponing our Lamentati
for the present, we hastily ran to the Dear You
and kneeling on each side of him implored h

t to die —. "Laura (said He fixing his now languid
s on me) I fear I have been overturned."
was overjoyed to find him yet sensible—.
"Oh! tell me Edward (said I) tell me I beseech you
re you die, what has befallen you since that
happy Day in which Augustus was arrested
we were separated—"

"I will "(said he) and instantly fetching a
p sigh, Expired—. Sophia immediately sunk
in into a swoon—. My Greif was more audible
Voice faltered, My Eyes assumed a vacant stare,
face became as pale as Death, and my Senses
e considerably impaired—.

"Talk not to me of Phaetons (said I, raving
a frantic, incoherent manner) —Give me a
lin—. I'll play to him & sooth him in his
lancholy Hours— Beware ye gentle Nymphs
Cupid's Thunderbolts, avoid the piercing Shafts
Jupiter— Look at that Grove of Firs— I see a
of Mutton— They told me Edward was not
d; but they deceived me— they took him for
cucumber—" Thus I continued wildly exclaiming

on my Death —. For two Hours did I race there
madly and should not then have left off, as I was
not in the least fatigued, had not Sophia who was
just recovered from her swoon, intreated me to
consider that Night was now approaching and
that the Damps began to fall. "And whither
shall we go (said I) to shelter us from either." —
"To that white Cottage." (replied she pointing to
a neat building which rose up amidst the grove
of Elms & which I had not before observed —) I a:
:greed & we instantly walked to it — we knocked
at the door — it was opened by an old Woman;
being requested to afford us a Night's Lodging, she
informed us that her House was but small, tho'
she had only two Bed rooms, but that However we
should be welcome to one of them. We were sat:
:fied & followed the good Woman into the House
where we were greatly cheered by the sight of a
comfortable fire —. She was a Widow & had
one Daughter, who was then just Seventeen;
One of the best of ages; but alas! she was

...y plain & her name was Bridget..... Nothing
...efore could be expected from her —- she could
...- be supposed to possess either exalted Ideas,
...licate Feelings or refined Sensibilities ——
... was nothing more than a mere good-
...mpered, civil & obliging Young Woman; as
...ch we could scarcely dislike her — she
... only an Object of Contempt—. Adieu
                              Laura —

...tter the 14th

   Laura in continuation

Arm yourself my amiable Young Freind with
the philosophy you are mistress of; summon
...ll the fortitude you possess, for alas! in the
...usal of the following Pages your sensibility
... be most severely tried. Ah! what were the
...sfortunes I had before experienced & which I have
...ady related to you, to the one I am now going
... inform you of! The Death of my Father and Mother
... my Husband though almost more than my
...le Nature could support, were trifles in com:
...ison to the misfortune I am now proceeding
                              to relate.

The morning after our arrival at the Cottage
Sophia complained of a violent pain in her delicate
limbs, accompanied with a disagreable Head-ake
She attributed it to a cold caught by her continual
faintings in the open air as the Dew was falling
the Evening before. This I feared was but too pro-
:bably the case; since how could it be otherwise
accounted for that I should have escaped the same
indisposition, but by supposing that the bodily
Exertions I had undergone in my repeated fits of
frenzy had so effectually circulated & warmed my
Blood as to make me proof against the chilling
Damps of Night, whereas, Sophia lying totally
inactive on the Ground must have been exposed
to all their Severity. I was most seriously a-
:larmed by her illness which trifling as it may
appear to you, a certain instinctive Sensibility
whispered me, would in the End be fatal to her

Alas! my fears were but too fully justified; she
grew gradually worse - & I daily became more
alarmed for her. — At length she was obliged to
confine herself solely to the Bed allotted us

by our worthy Landlady—. Her disorder turned
a galloping Consumption & in a few Days car:
d her off. Amidst all my Lamentations for
(& violent you may suppose they were) I
t received some consolation in the reflection
my having paid every Attention to her, that
to be offered, in her illness. I had wept over
every Day—had bathed her ~~fair~~ sweet face with
tears & had pressed her fair Hands continually
mine—. "My beloved Laura (said she to me
o Hours before she died) take warning from
unhappy End & avoid the imprudent conduct
ich has occasioned it... Beware of fainting fits...
ough at the time they may be refreshing & Agreable
beleive me they will in the end, if too often re:
ted & at improper seasons, prove destructive
ur Constitution... My fate will teach you this..
e a Martyr to my greif for the loss of Augustus..
fatal swoon has cost me my Life... Beware
swoons Dear Laura.... A frenzy fit is not one
ter so pernicious; it is an exercise to the

Body & if not too violent, is I dare say conducive to He
in its consequences — Run mad as often as you chu
but do not faint —".

These were the last ^words she ever addressed to m
It was her dieing Advice to her afflicted Laura, w
has ever most faithfully adhered to it.

After having attended my lamented freind to he
Early Grave, I immediately (tho' late at night) left
the detested Village ~~where~~ in which she died, & near which th
expired my Husband & Augustus. I had not walk
many yards from it before I was overtaken by a S
-Coach, in which I instantly took a place, determin
to proceed in it to Edinburgh, where I hoped to find s
kind some pitying Freind who would receive & com
-fort me in my Afflictions.

It was so dark when I entered the Coa
that I could not distinguish the Number of my
Fellow-travellers; I could only perceive that they
were many. Regardless however of any thing co
:cerning them, I gave myself up to my own sa
Reflections. A ~~natural~~ general Silence prevailed ——
~~only~~ — A Silence, which was by nothing interr
but by the loud & repeated Snores of one of the Par

28

"What an illiterate villain must that Man be." (thought myself) What a total Want of delicate refinement st he have, who can thus shock our senses such a brutal Noise! He must I am certain capable of every bad action! There is no crime black for such a Character!" Thus reasoned I ithin myself, & doubtless such were the re: ections of my fellow travellers.

At length, returning Day enabled me behold the unprincipled Scoundrel who had so ently disturbed my feelings. It was Sir Edward father of my Deceased Husband. By his Side, sate gusta, & on the same seat with me were your Mother Lady Dorothea. Imagine my surprise at finding yself thus seated amongst my old Acquaintance. eat as was my astonishment, it was yet in: ased, when on looking out of windows, I beheld the sband of Philippa, with Philippa by his side, on Coach-box, & when on looking behind I beheld, Phi: nder & Gustavus in the basket." Oh! Heavens, (ex: imed I) is it possible that I should so unexpect y be surrounded by my nearest Relations and nections." These words roused the rest of the Party.

and every eye was directed to the corner in which I
sat. "Oh! my Isabel (continued I throwing myself
a-cross Lady Dorothea into her arms) receive once
more to your bosom the unfortunate Laura. Alas
when we last parted in the Vale of Usk, I was
hap:py in being united to the best of Edwards; I had
then a Father & a Mother, & had never known mis
:fortunes — But now deprived of every friend but
you ——"

"What! (interrupted Augusta) is my Brother dead
then? Tell us I intreat you what is become of him."

"Yes, cold & insensible Nymph, (replied I) that luck
:less Swain your Brother, is no more, & you may
now glory in being the Heiress of Sir Edward's fortune."

Although I had always despised her from the day
I had overheard her conversation with my Edward,
yet in civility I complied with hers & Sir Edward's
intreaties that I would inform them of the whole
melancholy affair. They were greatly shocked —
Even the obdurate Heart of Sir Edward & the insen
:sible one of Augusta, were touched with sorrow at
the unhappy tale. At the request of your Mother

related to them every other misfortune which had
fallen me since we parted. Of the imprisonment
Augustus & the absence of Edward — of our arrival
Scotland — of our unexpected Meeting with our
Grandfather & our cousins — of our visit to Mac:
nald-Hall — of the singular Service we there performed
wards Janetta — of her Father's ingratitude for it....
his inhuman behaviour, unaccountable sus:
icions, & barbarous treatment of us, in obliging
to leave the House .... Of our Lamentations on
e loss of Edward & Augustus & finally of the me:
ncholy Death of my beloved Companion.

Pity & Surprise were strongly depictured in your
ther's Countenance, during the whole of my narra:
tion, but I am sorry to say, that to the eternal re:
roach of her Sensibility, the latter infinitely pre:
minated. Nay, faultless as my Conduct had cer:
inly been during the whole course of my late
isfortunes & Adventures, she pretended to find
lt with my Behaviour in many of the Situa:
ns in which I had been placed. As I was sensible
self, that I had always behaved in a manner
ch reflected Honour on my Feelings & Refinement, I paid

little attention to what she said, & desired her to
satisfy my curiosity by informing me how she
came there, instead of wounding my spotless
:putation with <ins>unjustifiable</ins> ~~unworthy~~ Reproaches. As soon
she had complyed with my wishes in this par
:ticular & had given me an accurate detail
every thing that had befallen her since our
separation (the particulars of which if you are not
already acquainted with, your Mother will give
I applied to Augusta for the same information
respecting herself, Sir Edward & Lady Dorothea

She told me that having a considerable taste
the Beauties of Nature, her curiosity to behold the
~~beautiful~~ <ins>delightful</ins> Scenes it exhibited in that part of
World had been so much raised by Gilpin's Tour
to the Highlands, that she had prevailed on her
Father to undertake a Tour to Scotland & had
persuaded Lady Dorothea to accompany them. Th
they had arrived at Edinburgh a few Days be
& from thence had ~~many~~ <ins>made</ins> daily Excursions in
the Country around in the Stage Coach they we
then in, from one of which Excursions they w
at that time returning - My next enquiries

morning Philippa & her Husband, the latter of
...m I learned having spent all her fortune, had
...urse for subsistence to the talent in which, he
...always most excelled, namely, Driving, &
...t having sold every thing which belonged to
...m except their Coach, had converted it into
...tage & in order to be removed from any of his
...mer Acquaintance, had driven it to Edinburgh
...m whence he went to Sterling every other
...y, That Philippa stile retaining her af:
...tion for her ungratefull Husband, had followed
...n to Scotland & always generally accompanied him
...his little Excursions to Sterling. "It has only
...n to throw a little money into their Pockets
...tinued Augusta) that my Father has always
...tted in their Coach to view the beauties of
...Country Since our arrival in Scotland — for
...would certainly have been much more agre:
...le to us, to visit the Highlands in a Post chaise
...n merely to travel from Edinburgh to Sterling
...om Sterling to Edinburgh every other Day in
...ouded & uncomfortable Stage." I perfectly

agreed with her in her sentiments on the aff
& secretly blamed Sir Edward for thus sacrifi
his Daughter's Pleasure for the sake of a ridic
old Woman whose folly in marrying so you
a Man ought to be punished. His behaviour
however was entirely of a peice with his ge
:ral Character; for what could be expected from
Man who possessed not the smallest atom of
Sensibility, who scarcely knew the meanin
Simpathy, & who actually Snored —. Adeiu
                              Laura.

Letter the 15th

            Laura in continuation.

        When we arrived at the town where we
were to Breakfast, I was determined to speak
with Philander & Gustavus, & to that purpo
as soon as I left the Carriage, I went to the
Basket & tenderly enquired after their Health
expressing my fears for the uneasiness of the
Situation. At first they seemed rather confus
at my appearance dreading no doubt that I
might call them to account for the money wh

Grandfather had left me & which they had un:
stly deprived me of, but finding that I remain:
ned nothing of the Matter, they desired me
step into the Basket as we might there con:
se with greater ease. Accordingly I entered
whilst the rest of the party were devouring
en tea & buttered toast, we feasted ourselves
a more refined & sentimental Manner by a
fidential Conversation. I informed them of
ry thing which had befallen me them during
 course of my Life, & at my request they related
me every incident of theirs.

"We are the sons as you already know, of the
 youngest Daughters which Lord St Clair had by
ria an italian opera-girl. Our mothers could
ther of them exactly ascertain who were our
thers; though it is generally believed that Phi:
der, is the son of one Philip Jones a Bricklayer
that my Father was Gregory Staves a Staymaker of
burgh. This is however of little consequence, for as
Mothers were certainly never married to either of them
eflects no Dishonour on our Blood, which is of a

most ancient & unpolluted kind. Bertha (the Mo
of Philander) & Agatha (my own Mother) always lived tog
They were neither of them very rich; their uni
fortunes had originally amounted to nine thousa
Pounds, but as they had always lived upon th
principal of it, when we were fifteen it wa
:minished to nine Hundred. This nine Hund
they always kept in a Drawer in one of the Tab
which stood in our common sitting Parlour, for t
convenience of having it always at hand. Whe
it was from this circumstance, of its being ea
taken, or from a wish of being independant, or f
an excess of Sensibility (for which we were alway
remarkable) I cannot now determine, but cer
:tain it is that when we had reached our 15th y
we took the Nine Hundred Pounds & ran away
Having obtained this prize we were determin
to manage it with economy & not to spend it ei
with folly or Extravagance. To this purpose w
therefore divided it into nine parcels, one of whi
we devoted to Victuals, the 2d to Drink, the 3 to h
-keeping, the 4th to Carriages, the 5th to Horses, th

Servants, the 7th to amusements the 8th to Cloakes
the 9th to Silver Buckles. Having thus arranged
Expences for two Months (for we expected
make the nine Hundred Pounds last as long)
hastened to London & had the good luck to spend
in 7 weeks & a Day which was 6 Days
er than we had intended. As soon as we had
happily disincumbered ourselves from the
ight of so much Money, we began to think of
turning to our Mothers, but accidentally hearing
                    starved to Death,
t they were both dead, we gave over the design
determined to engage ourselves to some strolling
pany of Players, as we had always a turn for
Stage. Accordingly we offered our Services to
were accepted; our Company was indeed
ten small, as it consisted only of the Manager
wife & ourselves, but there were fewer to pay
the only inconvenience attending it was the
rity of Plays which for want of People to fill
Characters, we could perform. -- We did not mind
fles however -- One of our most admired Per-
                                    :formances

was Macbeth, in which we were truly great.
Manager always played Banquo himself, his
Wife my Lady Macbeth, I did the Three Witch
& Philander acted all the rest. To say the tru
this tragedy was not only the Best, but the o
Play we ever performed; & after having acted
all over England, Ireland and Wales, we came
Scotland to exhibit it over the remainder of
Great Britain. We happened to quit be quar
:tered in that very Town, where you came an
met your Grandfather — We were in the Inn-y
when his Carriage entered & perceiving by the
Arms to whom it belonged, & knowing that
St Clair was our Grandfather, we agreed to en
:deavour to get something from him by disa
:ing the Relationship — You know how well
succeeded — Having obtained the two hundre
Pounds, we instantly left the Town leavin
our Manager & his Wife to act Macbeth by the
:selves, & took the road to Sterling, where we

ent our little fortune with great eclat. We are
returning to Edinburgh in order to get some
ferment in the Acting way; & such my Dear
sin is our History."

I thanked the amiable Youth for his enter:
ning Narration, & after expressing my Wishes for
ir Welfare & Happiness, left them in their little
itation & returned to my other Friends who impa:
tly expected me.

My Adventures are now ~~growing~~ drawing to a close
dearest Marianne; at least for the present.
When we arrived at Edinburgh Sir Edward told
that as the Widow of his Son, he desired I would
t from his Hands of four Hundred a year. I graci:
ly promised that I would, but could not help
rving that the unsympathetic baronet offered
more on account of my being the Widow of
ward than in being the refined & amiable
ra.

I took up my ~~lodging~~ Residence in a ro:
antic Village in the Highlands of Scotland, where
we ever since continued, & where I can unin:
rupted by unmeaning Visits, indulge in a

melancholy solitude, my unceasing Lamentations
the Death of my Father, my Mother, my Husband
& my Freind.

Augusta has been for several Years united
the Man of all others most suited to her; she
she became acquainted with him during her
in Scotland.

Sir Edward in hopes of gaining an Heir
his Title & Estate, at the same time married La
Dorothea—. His wishes have been answered.

Philander & Gustavus, after having raise
their reputation by their Performances in the
-atrical Line at Edinburgh, removed to Coven
Garden, where they still continue to Exhibit
under the assumed names of Lewis & Quic

Philippa has long paid the Debt of Natu
Her Husband however still continues to
the Stage-Coach from Edinburgh to Sterling
Adeiu my Dearest Marianne.

Laura—

Finis

June 13th 1790

To Henry Thomas Austen Esqre —.

Sir

I am now availing myself of the Liberty you have frequently honoured me with of dedicating one of my Novels to you. That it is unfinished, I grieve; yet fear that from me, it will _{always} remain so; that as far as it ^{is} carried, it could be so trifling and so unworthy of you, is

  another concern to your obliged humble
     Servant
     The Author

Messrs Demand & Co — please to pay Jane Austen Spinster the sum of one hundred guineas on account of your Humble Servant.
     H T Austen.

£105 : 0 . 0

Lesley Castle

an unfinished Novel in Letters.

Letter The first is from

Miss Margaret Lesley to Miss Charlotte Luth[

Lesley Castle Jan 3d -1

My Brother has just left us. "Matilda (sai
he at parting) you and Margaret will I am certai
take all the care of my dear little one, that she
might have received from an indulgent, an affection
an amiable Mother." Tears rolled down his chee
as he spoke these words — the remembrance of he
who had so wantonly disgraced the Maternal ch
-racter and so openly violated the conjugal Duties,
prevented his adding anything farther; he emb
his sweet Child and after saluting Matilda & M
hastily broke from us — and seating himself in h
Chaise, pursued the road to Aberdeen. Never wa

a better young Man! ah! how little did

deserve the misfortunes he has experienced

the Marriage state. So good a Husband to so bad

ife; for you know my dear Charlotte that the

thless Louisa left him, her Child & reputation

weeks ago in company with Danvers & dishonour

ir was there a sweeter face, a finer form, or a

amiable Heart than Louisa owned! Her child

dy possesses the personal Charms of her un-

ppy Mother! May she inherit from her Father

his mental ones! Lesley is at present but five

twenty, and has already given himself up to

ncholy and Despair; what a difference between

and his Father; Sir George is 57 and still remains

Beau, the flighty stripling, the gay Lad, and sprightly

Rakehelly Dishonor Esqre

Youngster, that his Son was really about five y
back, and that he has affected to appear f ever
since my remembrance. While our father is f
-tering about the streets of London, gay, dissipa
and Thoughtless at the age of 57, Matilda and
contence secluded from Mankind in our old an
Mouldering Castles which is situated two mile
from Perth on a bold projecting Rock, and comm
an extensive view of the Town and its delightf
Environs. But tho' retired from almost all the
World, (for we visit no one but the McLeods, The
McKenzies, the McPhersons, the McCartneys, the Mcd
The McKinnons, the McLellans, the McKays, the
Macbeths and the Macduffs) we are neither d
nor unhappy; on the contrary there never were
more lively, more agreable or more witty girls, th
we are; not an hour in the Day hangs hea

our hands. We read, we work, we walk, and
n fatigued with these Employments releive
spirits, either by a lively song, a graceful
e, or by some smart bon-mot, and witty repartee.
re handsome my dear Charlotte, very handsome
the greatest of our Perfections is, that we
entirely insensible of them ourselves. But why
I thus dwell on myself? Let me rather re-
t the praise of our dear little Neice the inno-
t Louisa, who is at present sweetly smiling
a gentle Nap, as she reposes on the Sofa. The
Creature is just turned of two years old; as
dsome as tho' 2 & 20, as sensible as tho' 2 & 30,
as prudent as tho' 2 & 40. To convince you of
I must inform you that she has a very fine

complexion and very pretty features, that she al
-ready knows the two first Letters in the Alphabet
and that she never tears her frocks –. If I have
now convinced you of her Beauty, Sense & Pruden
I have nothing more to urge in support of my q
:tion, and you will therefore have no way of de
:ding the Affair but by coming to Lesley - casth
and by a personal acquaintance with Louisa, d
-termine for yourself. Ah! my dear Freind, how h
should I be to see you within these venerable Wa
It is now four years since my removal from so
has separated me from you; that ~~to~~ two such tender
Hearts, so closely linked together by the ties of su
: pathy and Friendship, should be so widely un
from each other. is vastly moving. I live in

...rthshire, You in Sussex. We might meet in
...don, were my Father disposed to carry me
...e, and were your Mother to be there at the
...e time. We might meet at Bath, at Tunbridge,
...any where else indeed, could we but be at the
...e place together. We have only to hope that
...h a period may arrive. My Father does not
...in to us till Autumn; my Brother will leave
...land in a few Days; he is impatient to travel.
...staken Youth! He vainly flatters himself that
...nge of air will heal the Wounds of a broken
...rt! You will join with me I am certain my
...r Charlotte, in prayers for the recovery of the
...happy Lesley's peace of Mind, which must ever
...sential to that of your sincere friend M. Lesley.

Letter the second

From Miss C. Lutterell to Miss M. Lesley in answ

Glenford   Feb:ry 12

I have a thousand excuses to beg for having

so long delayed thanking you my dear Pegg

for your agreeable Letter, which beleive me I sh

not have deferred doing, had not every momer

of my time during the last five weeks beer

fully employed in the necessary arrangemen

for my sisters Wedding, as to allow me no tir

to devote either to you or myself. And now wha

provokes me more than any thing else is tha

the Match is broke off, and all my Labour thr

away: Imagine how great the Dissapointment m

be to me, when you consider that after having

...toured both by Night and by Day, in order to get

... Wedding dinner ready by the time appointed,

... having roasted Beef, Broiled Mutton, and

... Soup enough to last the new married Couple

... the Honey-moon, ~~to find that~~ *I had the* mortification

... finding that I had been Roasting, Broiling

... Stewing both the Meat and Myself to no

...pose. Indeed my dear Friend, I never remem-

... suffering any vexation equal to what I

...enced on last Monday. when my Sister came

...ning to me in the Store-room with her face

...White as a Whipt syllabub, and told me that

...uey had been thrown from his Horse, had

...tured his Scull and was pronounced by his Sur-

... to be in the most emminent Danger.

"Good God! (said I) you dont say so? why what
in the name of Heaven will become of all the
Victuals!" We shall never be able to eat it while
it is good. However, we'll call in the Surgeon
help us—. I shall be able to manage the Sir-lo
myself; my Mother will eat the soup, and You
and the Docter must finish the rest." Here I
was interrupted, by seeing my poor Sister fall
down to appearance Lifeless upon one of the
Chests, where we keep our Table linen. I im-
-mediately called my Mother and the Maids, an
at last we brought her to herself again; as so
as ever she was sensible, she expressed a de
                    instantly
-termination of going to Henry, and was so wa
bent on this Scheme, that we had the greatest
Difficulty in the World to prevent her putting

...ention; at last however more by Force than En-
...aty we prevailed on her to go into her room;
...tt we laid her upon the Bed, and she continued
some Hours in the most dreadful Convulsions. My
...other and I continued in the room with her,
...d when any intervals of tolerable Composure
Eloisa would allow us, we joined in heartfelt
...entations on the dreadful Waste in our provisions which this
...nt must occasion, and in concerting some
...n for getting rid of them. We agreed that the
...t thing we could do was to begin eating them
...mediately, and accordingly we ordered up the
Ham and Fowls, and instantly began our
...ouring Plan on them with great alacrity. We
...d have persuaded Eloisa to have taken a Wing
...a Chicken, but she would not be persuaded. The

was however much quieter than she had been
the Convulsions she had before suffered having given
way to an almost perfect Insensibility. We en-
-deavoured to rouse her by every means in our
power, but to no purpose. I talked to her of Henry
"Dear Eloisa (said I) there's no occasion for your
crying so much about such a trifle. (for I was
willing to make light of it in order to comfort her)
I beg you would not mind it — You see it does not
vex me in the least; though perhaps I may suffer
                from
most fit it after all; for I shall not only be obliged
to eat up all the Victuals I have dressed already
but must if Henry should recover (which however
is not very likely) dress as much for you again

should he die (as I suppose he will) I shall still
...e to prepare a Dinner for you whenever you
...ry any one else. So you see that tho' perhaps
the present it may afflict you to think of
...ny's sufferings, yet I dare say he'll die soon,
...then his pain will be over and you will be
..., whereas my Trouble will last much longer
work as hard as I may, I am certain that
pantry cannot be cleared in less than a fort:
...ight." Thus I did all in my power to con—
...le her, but without any effect, and at last as
...saw that she did not seem to listen to me, I
                    but leaving
...d no more, ~~Xxxx~~ her with my Mother ~~and~~ I
...h
...down the remains of the Ham & Chicken,

and sent William to ask how Hervey did. He
not expected to live many Hours; he died the
same day. We took all possible care to break
Melancholy ~~Account~~ Event to Eloisa in the tenderest m
:ner; yet in spite of every precaution, her suffe
on hearing it were too violent for her reason, a
She continued for many hours in a high Deliric
She is still extremely ill, and her Physicians
greatly afraid of her going into a Decline. We
therefore preparing for Bristol, where we mean
be in the course of the next week. And now
dear Margaret let me talk a little of your af
:fairs; and in the first place I must inform
that it is confidently reported, your Father is
to be married; I am very unwilling to believe

...leasing a report, and at the same time cannot
...ly discredit it. I have written to my friend
...an Fitzgerald, for information concerning it, which
...she is at present in Town, she will be very
...e to give me. I know not who is the Lady.
...think your Brother is extremely right in the
...olution he has taken of travelling, as it will
...haps contribute to obliterate from his remem-
...nce, those disagreable Events, which have
...tily so much afflicted him— I am happy to
...d that tho' secluded from all the World, neither
...nor Matilda are dull or unhappy— that you
...y never know what it is to be either is the
...ish of your Sincerely Affectionate C.L.

P.S. I have this instant received an answer

from my friend Susan, which I enclose to you,
on which you will make your own reflections.

The enclosed Letter

My dear Charlotte

You could not have applied for infor
tion concerning the report of Sir George Lesley
Marriage, to any one better able to give it you
than I am. Sir George is certainly married; I w
myself present at the Ceremony, which you wi
not be surprised at when I subscribe myself yo
affectionate Susan Lesley

Letter the third

From Miss Margaret Lesley to Miss C. Lutter
Lesley Castle February the 16th

I have made my own reflections on the le

enclosed to me, my Dear Charlotte and I will now
~ you what those reflections were. I reflected that ~
~ this second Marriage Sir George should have a
~ family, our fortunes must be considerably
~ minished — that if his Wife should be of an ex-
~ vagant turn, she would encourage him to persevere
~ that Gay & Dissipated way of Life to which little
~ couragement would be necessary, and which has I
~ already proved but too detrimental to his
~lth and fortune — that she would now become
~ stress of those Jewels which once adorned our
~ ther, and which Sir George had always promised
~ that if they did not come into Perthshire
~ould not be able to gratify my curiosity of behold-
~ my Mother-in-law, and that if they did, Matilda

would no longer sit at the head of her Father's
:ble—. These my dear Charlotte were the melan=
:choly reflections which crowded into my imagin
after perusing Susan's letter to you, and which
:stantly occurred to Matilda when she had peru=
it likewise. The same ideas, the same fears,
:mediately occupied her Mind, and I know not wh=
reflection distressed her most, whether the probab=
Diminution of our Fortunes, or her own Conseq=
We both wish very much to know whether
Lady Lesley is handsome & what is your opin=
of her; as you honour her with the appellation
of your friend, we flatter ourselves that she m=
be amiable. My Brother is already in Par=

intends to quit it in a few Days, and to begin

route to Italy. He writes in a most chearfull Man-

, says that the air of France has greatly

ned both his Health and Spirits; that he

now entirely ceased to think of Louisa with

y degree either of Pity or Affection, that he even

ls himself obliged to her for her Elopement, as

thinks it very good fun to be single again.

this, you may perceive that he has entirely

ned that chearful Gaiety, and sprightly Wit,

which he was once so remarkable. When he

t became acquainted with Louisa which was

he more than three years ago, he was one of

most lively, the most agreable young Man of

the age—. I beleive you never yet heard the partic-

:lars of his first acquaintance with her. It com-

:menced at our cousin Colonel Drummond's;

whose house in Cumberland he spent the Christ

:mas, in which he attained the age of two and

twenty. Louisa Burton was the Daughter of a

distant Relation of Mrs Drummond, who dieing

a few Months before in extreme poverty, left her

only Child then about eighteen to the protection

of any of his Relations who would protect her

Mrs Drummond was the only one who found

herself so disposed—Louisa was therefore re

:moved from a miserable Cottage in Yorkshire to

an elegant Mansion in Cumberland; and fur

...ny pecuniary Distress that Poverty could inflict,
...ny elegant Enjoyment that Money could pur:
...ase—. Louisa was naturally ill-tempered and
...ning; but she had been taught to disguise
...real Disposition, under the appearance of
...nuating Sweetness, by a father who but too
...ll knew, that to be married, would be the only
...nce she would have of not being starved, and
...o flattered himself that with such an ex:
...ordinary share of personal beauty, joined to
...gentleness of Manners, and an engaging address,
...might stand a good chance of pleasing some
...ng Man who might afford to marry a
...l without a Shilling. Louisa perfectly entered

into her father's schemes and was determined
to forward them with all her care & attention.
By dint of Perseverance and application, she
had at length so thoroughly disguised her na-
:tural disposition under the mask of Innocence
and Softness, as to impose upon every one who
had not by a long and constant intimacy with
her discovered her real Character. Such was
Louisa when the hapless Lesley first beheld
her at Drummond-house. His heart which
(to use your favourite comparison) was as
delicate as sweet and as tender as a whipt
-syllabub, could not resist her attractions. In
a very few Days, he was falling in love

...tly after actually fell, and before he had

...own her a Month, he had married her. My

...her was at first highly displeased at so

...ty and imprudent a connection; but when

...found that they did not mind it, he soon

...ame perfectly reconciled to the match. The

...te near Aberdeen which my brother possesses

...the bounty of his great Uncle independant

...ir George, was entirely sufficient to sup-

...t him and my Sister in Elegance & Ease.

...the first twelvemonth, no one could be hap:

...than Lesley, and no one more amiable to

...earance than Louisa, and so plausibly did

she act and so cautiously behave that M[...]
Matilda and I often spent several weeks t[...]
with them, yet we neither of us had any s[...]
:picion of her real Disposition. After the b[...]
of Louisa however, which one would have t[...]
would have strengthened her regard for Jes[...]
the mask she had so long supported was [...]
degrees thrown aside, and as probably s[...]
then thought herself secure in the affecti[...]
of her Husband (which did indeed appea[...]
if possible augmented by the birth of his [...]
she seemed to take no pains to prevent [...]
affection from ever diminishing. Our visi[...]
therefore to Dunbeath, were now less frequ[...]

by far less agreable than they used to be.

absence was however never either mentioned

lamented by Louisa who in the society of young

vers with whom she became acquainted at

deen (he was at one of the Universities

,) felt infinitely happier than in that of

tilda and your freind, tho' there certainly never

e pleasanter Girls than we are. You know

sad end of all Lesleys connubial hap:

iness; I will not repeat it —. Adieu my

Charlotte; although I have not yet men:

ned any thing of the matter, I hope you will

me the justice to beleive that I think and

l, a great deal for your Sisters afflictions. I

do not doubt but that the healthy air of

the Bristol downs will intirely remove it,

by erasing from her Mind the remembrance

of Henry. I am my dear Charlotte y.^{rs} ever

ML —

Letter the fourth

From Miss C. Lutterele to Miss M. Lesley

Bristol February 27.th —

My dear Peggy

I have but just received your letter,

being directed to Sussex while I was at Bri

was obliged to be forwarded to me here, & f

some unaccountable Delay, has but this in

stant reached me .. I return you many th

for the account it contains of Lesley's ac

...ce, Love & Marriage with Louisa; which has not

...less entertained me for having often been

...ated to me before.

I have the satisfaction of informing you

...t we have every reason to imagine our

...try is by this time nearly cleared, as we

...t particular orders with the servants to

...t as hard as they possibly could, and to call

...a couple of Chairwomen to assist them. We

...ght a cold Pigeon-pye, a cold turkey, a cold

...e, and half a dozen Jellies with us, which

...were lucky enough with the help of our

...dlady, her husband, and their three chil:

...n, to get rid of, in less than two days after

our arrival. Poor Eloisa is still so very in
:ferent both in Health & Spirits, that I very
much fear, the air of the Bristol downs, h
as it is, has not been able to drive poor
Henry from her remembrance.

You ask me whether your new
Mother inlaw is handsome & ameable. I
now give you an exact description of her b
and mental charms. She is short, and ex
:ly well-made; is naturally pale, but rou
a good deal; has fine eyes, and fine teeth,
She will take care to let you know as soon
she sees you, and is altogether very pre
She is remarkably good-tempered when

her own way, and very lively when she is
out of humour. She is naturally extrava:
t and not very affected; she never reads
thing but the letters she receives from me,
never writes anything but her answers
hem. She plays, sings & Dances, but has
taste for either, and excells in none, tho'
says she is passionately fond of all. Perhaps
may flatter me so far as to be surprised
one of whom I speak with so little affec:
should be my particular friend; but to tell
the truth, our friendship arose rather from
                her side,
e on herself than Esteem on mine. We spent
three days together with a Lady in Berkshire

with whom we both happened to be connected.
During our visit, the weather being remarkably
bad, and our party particularly stupid, she
was so good as to conceive a violent ~~friendship~~ *partiality* for
me, which very soon ~~settled~~ in a downright
Freindship, and ended in an established cor
:pondence. She is probably by this time as tir
of me as I am of her; but as she is too
polite and I am too civil to say so, our lett
are still as frequent and affectionate as eve
and our attachment as firm and sincere a
when it ~~was~~ first commenced.—As she has a
great taste for the pleasures of London, and the am
~~ments~~ of Brighthelmstone, she will I dare say

e difficulty in prevailing on herself even to satisfy

curiosity ~~~~~~~~ I dare say she feels of beholding you,

the expence of quitting those favourite haunts

dissipation, for the melancholy tho' venerable

m of the castle you inhabit. Perhaps however

he finds her health impaired by too much a-

sement, she may acquire fortitude sufficient to

take a Journey to Scotland in the hope of its prov:

at least beneficial to her health, if not conducive

ir happiness. Your fears I am sorry to say, con:

ing your father's extravagance, your own fortunes,

– Mothers Jewels and your sister's consequence, I

d suppose are but too well founded. My friend

lf has four thousand pounds, and will proba

: bly

spend nearly as much every year in Dress
Public places, if she can get it — she will cert.
not endeavour to reclaim Sir George from the
:ner of living to which he has been solong
:customed, and there is therefore some reas.
fear that you will be very well off, if y
get any fortune at all. The Jewels I sho
imagine too will undoubtedly be hers, & the
is too much reason to think that she will
preside at her Husbands table in preferen
to his Daughter. But as so melancholy a
subject must necessarily extremely distress y
I will no longer dwell on it. —

...a's indisposition has brought us to Bristol

...so unfashionable a season of the year, that

...have actually seen but one genteel family

...we came. M.r & M.rs Marlowe are very

...able people; the ill health of their little boy

...sioned their arrival here; you may imagine

...being the only family with whom we can

...urse, we are of course on a footing of intima-

...ith them; we see them indeed almost every

...and dined with them yesterday. We spent a

pleasant Day, and had a very good Dinner,

to be sure the Veal was terribly underdone,

the Curry had no seasoning. I could not help

wishing all dinner-time that I had been
the dressing it. A brother of Mrs. Marlowe, Mr.
Cleveland is with them at present; he is a
good-looking young Man, and seems to have
a good deal to say for himself. I tell Eloisa
she should set her cap at him, but she does
not at all seem to relish the proposal. I should
like to see the girl married and Cleveland has
a very good estate. Perhaps you may wonder
that I do not consider myself as well as my
Sister in my matrimonial Projects; but to tell
you the truth I never wish to act a more, prin-
-cipal part at a Wedding than the super-

...ding and directing the Dinner, and therefore

acquaintance

...le I can get any of my ~~friends~~ to marry

me, I shall never think of doing it my:

...t, as I very much suspect that I should

have so much time for dressing my own

...ing dinner, as for dressing that of my

...ds. Yrs sincerely   CL.

Letter the fifth

to

...iss Margaret Lesley ~~and~~ Miss Charlotte Lutterell

Lesley – Castle March 18th

On the same day that I received your last

...d letter, Matilda received one from Sir George

which was dated from Edinburgh, and infor

us that he should do himself the pleasure

introducing Lady Lesley to us on the follow

evening. This as you may suppose consi-

:bly surprised us, particularly as your acco

of her Ladyship had given us reason to im:

~~that~~ there was little chance of her visiti

Scotland at a time that London must be

gay. As it was our business however to

delighted at such a mark of condescensi

as a visit from Sir George and Lady Lesley,

prepared to return them an answer expre

the happiness we enjoyed in expectation of such

Blessing, when luckily recollecting that as they

to reach the Castle the next Evening, it

ld be impossible for my father to receive

before he left Edinburgh, We ~~therefore~~ con:

ted ourselves with leaving them to suppose

t we were as happy as we ought to be.

nine in the Evening on the following

they came, accompanied by one of Lady

ys brothers. Her Ladyships perfectly answers

description you sent me of her, except that

I do not think her so pretty as you seem to
consider her. She has not a bad face, but there
is something so extremely unmajestic in her
little diminutive figure, as to render her in
         with
comparison ~~to~~ the elegant height of Matilda
and Myself, an insignificant Dwarf. Her
curiosity to see us (which must have been
         bring her
great to ~~have brought us~~ more than four
hundred miles) being now perfectly grat
ified, she already begins to mention their
to town, and has desired us to accompany
her.. We cannot refuse her request since

seconded by the commands of our Father, and

ded by the entreaties of W.^r Fitzgerald who

tainly one of the most pleasing young Men,

er beheld. It is not yet determined when

are to go, but when ever we do we shall cer:

ily take our little Louisa with us. Adieu

dear Charlotte; Matilda unites in best

es to you & Eloisa, with yours ever ML

Letter the sixth

dy Lesley to Miss Charlotte Luttrell

Lesley-castle March 20.th

arrived here my sweet Freind about a

fortnight ago, and I already heartily repent tha

I ever left our charming House in Portman-Squ

for such a dismal old weather-beaten Castle as

this. You can form no idea sufficiently hideou

of its dungeon-like ~~appearance~~ form. It is actual

to appearance

perched upon a Rock so ~~totally~~ inaccessible, th

I expected to have been pulled up by a rope; a

Sincerely repented having gratified my curiosity

to behold my Daughters at the expence of bein

obliged to enter their prison in so dangerous

ridiculous a Manner. But as soon as I one

...nd myself safely arrived in the inside of this ...mendous building, I comforted myself with the ...e of having my spirits revived, by the sight ... two beautifull girls, such as the Miss Lesleys had ...n represented to me, at Edinburgh. But here ...in, I met with nothing but Disapointment ...d Surprise. Matilda and Margaret Lesley ... two great, tall, out of the way, over-grown, ...ls, just of a proper size to inhabit a Castle ...ost as Large in comparison as themselves. ...ish my dear Charlotte that you could but behold these scotch giants; I am sure they would

frighten you out of your wits. They will do

well as foils to myself, so I have invited them

to accompany me to London where I hope to

in the course of a fortnight. Besides these to

fair Damsels, I found a little humoured Bra

here who I believe is some relation to the

they told me who she was, and gave me

long rigmarole story of her father and a

Somebody which I have entirely forgot. I ha

Scandal and detest Children. — I have been p

gued ever since I came here with tiresome vis

a parcel of Scotch wretches, with terrible

names: they were so civil, gave me so many

itations, and talked of coming again so soon,

t I could not help affronting them. I suppose

ll not see them any more, and yet as a

ily party we are so stupid, that I do not

w what to do with myself. These girls

no Music, but Scotch airs, no Drawings

Scotch Mountains, and no Books but

h Poems — and I hate every thing Scotch.

eneral I can spend half the Day at my toilette

a great deal of pleasure; but why should I dress

here, since there is not a creature in the House
whom I have any wish to please. — I have just
had a conversation with my Brother in which
he has greatly offended me, and which as I
have nothing more entertaining to send you
I will give you the particulars of. You must
know that I have for these 4 or 5 Days past
strongly suspected William of entertaining a
partiality for my eldest Daughter. I own indeed
that had I been inclined to fall in love with
any woman, I should not have made choice of
Matilda Lesley for the object of my passion,
there is nothing I hate so much as a tall

man: but however there is no accounting

some men's taste and as William is himself

ly six feet high, it is not wonderful that

should be partial to that height. Now as I

a very great affection for my Brother

should be extremely sorry to see him un-

apy, which I suppose he means to be if he

not marry Matilda, as moreover I know

his Circumstances will not allow him

marry any one without a fortune, and that

da's is entirely dependant on her Father,

will neither have his own inclination

nor my permission to give her any thing at
:sent, I thought it would be doing a good
:natured action by my Brother to let him
know as much, in order that he might
                                                    his
choose for himself, whether to conquer ~~her~~,
:sion, or Love and Despair. Accordingly findin
myself this Morning alone with him in one
the horrid old rooms of this Castle, I opened the
cause to him in the following Manner.

" Well my dear William what do you think
these girls? for my part, I do not find the
so plain as I expected: but perhaps you may

...k me partial to the Daughters of my Husband

perhaps you are right – They are indeed

...y like Sir George that it is natural

think ......

...ny Dear Susan (cried he in a tone of the

...test amazement) you do not really

...ik they bear the least resemblance

...eir Father! He is so very plain! – but

...y your pardon – I had entirely forgotten

...hom I was speaking – "

...h! pray dont mind me; (replied I) every...

...knows Sir George is horribly ugly, and I

...re you I always thought him a fright."

...you surprise me extremely (answered Willi-

am)

by what you say both with respect to
Sir George and his Daughters. You can
think your Husband so deficient in p-
-sonal Charms as you speak of, nor c-
you surely see any resemblance betw-
him and the Miss Lesleys who are in
opinion perfectly unlike him & perf-
Handsome."

"If that is your opinion with rega-
to the girls it certainly is no proof of
Fathers beauty, for if they are perfe-
unlike him and very handsome at
same time, it is natural to supp-
that he is very plain."

no means, (said he) for what may be

ty in a Woman, may be very unpleasing

a Man."

"But you yourself (replied I) but a few

inutes ago allowed him to be very plain."

Men are no Judges of Beauty in their

Sex." (said he)

Neither Men nor Women can think Sir

ge tolerable."

Well, well, (said he) we will not dispute

ut his Beauty, but your opinion of his

ghters is surely very singular, for if I

stood you right, you said that you did not

them so plain as you expected to do."

"Why; do you find them plainer then." (said I)

"I can scarcely beleive you to be serio:
(returned he) when you speak of their,
:sons in so extraordinary a Manner.
not you think ~~that~~ the Miss Lesleys
two very handsome young Women?"

"Lord! No! (cried I) I think them terribly
plain!"

"Plain! (replied He) My dear Susan, you
cannot really think so! Why what si
Feature in the face of either of them, can
possibly find fault with?"

'Oh! trust me for that; (replied I).
I will begin with the eldest — with Mat
Shall I, William?" (I looked as cunni
as I could when I said it, inorder to

[come him.)

"They are so much alike (said he) that
[w]ould suppose the faults of one, would
[be] the faults of both."

"Well, then, in the first place, they are
[bo]th so horribly tall!"

"They are taller than you are indeed."
[sai]d he with a saucy smile.)

[N]ay, (said I) I know nothing of that"

[we]ll, but (he continued) tho' they may be
[abov]e the common size, their figures are
[perfec]tly elegant; and as to their faces, their
[eyes] are beautifull."

[I] never can think such tremendous,

knock-me-down figure in the least deg.
elegant, and as for their eyes, they are
fall that I never could strain my ne
enough to look at them."

"Nay, (replied he) I know not whether y
may not be in the right in not atten
it, for perhaps they might dazzle you w
their Lustre."

"Oh! Certainly. (said I, with the greate
complacency, for I assure you my deares
Charlotte that I was not in the least off
tho' by what followed, one would suppo
that William was conscious of having
me just cause to be so, for coming up to
and taking my hand, he said) "You n

t look so grave Susan; you will make

fear I have offended you.'"

ffended me! Dear Brother, how came

h a thought in your head! (returned I)

ually! I assure you that I am not in

t least surprised at your being so warm

advocate for the Beauty of these girls"

well, but (interrupted William) remember

t we have not yet concluded our dispute

erning them. What fault do you find

th their complexion?"

They are so horridly pale."

hey have always a little colour, & after

y exercise it is considerably heightened."

"Yes, but if there should ever happen to
be any rain in this part of the world, it
will never be able raise more than the
common stock — except indeed they amuse
themselves with running up & Down the
horrid old galleries and Antichambers —

"Well, (replied my Brother in a tone of
vexation, & glancing an impertinent Jeer
at me) if they have but little colour
at least, it is all their own."

This was too much my dear Charles
for I am certain that he tried the impu=
=dence by that look, of pretending to suspect
the reality of mine. But you I am sure
will vindicate my character whenever you

y hear it so cruelly aspersed, for you can

up how often I have protested against

ing Rouge, and how much I always told

I disliked it. And I assure you that my

ions are still the same. — Well, not
                        so
ing to be suspected by my Brother, I

the room immediately, and have been

since in my own Dressing-room writing

ow. What a long Letter have I made of it.

you must not expect to receive such

me when I get to Town; for it is only

Lesley castle, that one has time to write

to a Charlotte Luttrell. — I was so much

d by William's glance, that I could not

mon Patience enough, to stay & give him

that Advice respecting his Attachment
Matilda which had first induced me
pure Love to him to begin the convers:
and I am now so thoroughly convince
it, of his violent passion for her, that
am certain he would never hear re
on the Subject, and I shall therefore
myself no more trouble either about
him or his favourite. Adieu my dear
&r affectionately Susan Z

Letter the seventh
From Miss C. Luttrell to Miss M. Ler
Bristol the 27th of

I have received Letters from You & your Mo
in-law within this week which have grea
entertained me, as I find by them that your

th downright jealous of each others Beauty.

s very odd that two pretty Women tho' actually

ther & Daughter cannot be in the same

se without falling out about their faces.

be convinced that you are both perfectly

dsome and say no more of the Matter. I sup:

e ~~think~~ this Letter must be directed to

tman Square where probably (great as is your

ction for Lesley Castle) you will not be sorry

find yourself. In spite of all that People may

about Green fields and the Country I was al:

s of opinion that London and its Amusements

t be very agreable for a while, and should

ry happy could my Mother's income allow

                            its
to jockey us into her Public-places, during

Winter. I always longed particularly to go

Vaux-hall, to see whether the cold Beef

is cut so thin as it is reported, for I ha

sly suspicion that few people understo

the art of cutting a slice of cold Beef

well as I do: nay it would be hard if

not know something of the matter, for

that I took by

a part of my Education, ~~I always took~~

pains with. Mama always found me

best Scholar, tho' when Papa was alive

was his. Never to be sure were there two

different Dispositions in the World. We b

loved Reading. She preferred Histories, &

Receipts. She loved drawing Pictures, and

...wing Pullets. No one could sing a better song

...n She, and no one make a better Pye than

has

...nd so it always continued since we have

no longer children. The only difference is that

...disputes on the superior excellence of our

...loyments then so frequent are now no more.

...have for many years entered into an agree

...nt always to admire each other's works;

...ver fail listening to her Music, & she is

constant in eating my pies. Such at

...t was the case till Henry Hervey made

...appearance in Sussex. Before the ar:

...al of his Aunt in our neighbourhood

...e she establish'd herself you know

about a twelvemonth ago, his visits to her

been at stated times, and of equal *y* settled D

:tion; but on her removal to the Hall wh

is within a walk from our House, they

:came both more frequent & longer. This

you may suppose could not be pleasing to

Mrs Diana who is a professed enemy to

every thing which is not directed by Dec

and Formality, or which bears the least

:semblance to Ease and Good-breeding. Nay s

great was her aversion to her Nephews behav

that I have often heard her give such hints

it before his face that had not Henry at ju

...s been engaged in conversation with

...isa, they must have caught his Attention

...have very much distressed him. The altera:

...e in my sisters behaviour which I have before

...ted at, now took place. The Agreement we had

...ed into of admiring each others productions

...no longer seemed to regard, & tho' I constantly

...lauded even every Country-dance, She play'd,

...not even a pidgeon-pye of my making

                                        approbation.

...obtain from her a single word of ~~Praise~~

...was certainly enough to put any one in

...Passion; however, I was as cool as a Cream-

...se and having formed my plan & conceited

...heme of Revenge, I was determined to let

her have her own way & not even to make

a single reproach. My scheme was to treat

her as she treated me, and tho' she might

draw my own Picture or play Malbrook (whic

is

~~was~~ the only tune I ever really liked) not to

say so much as "Thank you Eloisa", tho' I had

many years constantly hollowed whenever s

played, Bravo, Braussimo, Encora, Da Capo, al

con espressione', and Poco presto with many oth

such outlandish words, all of them as Eloisa

me expressive of my Admiration; and so indee

suppose they are, as I see some of them in ev

Page of every Music book, being the Sentime

I imagine of the Composer.

I executed my Plan with great Punctu

n not say success, for alas! my silence while

...layed seemed not in the least to displease

...on the contrary she actually said to me one day

...e Charlotte, I am very glad to find that

...have at last left off that ridiculous cus-

...of applauding my Execution on the Harpsi-

...d till you made my head ake, & yourself

...o. I feel very much obliged to you for keep-

...your Admiration to yourself." I never shall

...t the very witty answer I made to this speech.

...isa (said I) I beg you would be quite at your

... with respect to all such fears in future, for

...sured that I shall always keep my Admiration

...yself & my own pursuits & never extend it

...rs." This was the only very severe

...I ever said in my Life; not but that I have

often felt myself extremely satirical but it

the only time I ever made my feelings public

I suppose there never were two young p

who had a greater affection for each other th

Henry & Eloisa; no, the Love of your Brother

Miss Burton could not be so strong tho' it

be more violent. You may imagine theref

how provoked my Sister must have bee

to have him play her such a trick. Poor gi

She still laments his Death, with undimi

:ed Constancy, notwithstanding he has been

more than six weeks; but some people min

such things more than others. The ill state

Health into which his Loss has thrown h

makes her so weak, & so unable to support

least exertion, that she has been in tears

is Morning mealy from having taken leave
of M.rs Marlowe who with her Husband, Brother
& Child are to leave Bristol this Morning.
I am sorry to have them go because they are the
family with whom we have here any ac:
=quintance; but I never thought of crying; to
me Eloisa & M.rs Marlowe have always been
more together than with me, and have therefore
acted a kind of affection for each other, which does
make Tears so inexcusable in them as they
would be in me. The Marlowes are going to Town,
& Cleveland accompanies them; as neither Eloisa
nor I could catch him I hope you or Matilda
may have better Luck. I know not when we
shall leave Bristol, Eloisa's Spirits are so low

that she is very averse to moving, and yet
certainly by no means amended by her residen[ce]
here. A week or two will I hope determin[e]
our Measures — in the mean time beleive m[e]
&c &c — Charlotte Luttre[ll]

Letter the Eighth

Miss Luttrell to Mrs Marlowe.

Bristol April 4th

I feel myself greatly obliged to you my
Emma for such a mark of your affection as
flatter myself was conveyed in the proposal
made me of our Corresponding; I assure you th[at]
it will be a great releif to me to write to [you]
and as long as my Health & Spirits will
me, you will find me a very constant corre
:dent; I will not say an entertaining one, for

— my situation sufficiently not to be ignorant

— in me Mirth would be improper & I know

too well not

— own Heart ~~well enough~~ to be sensible that

— ould be unnatural. You must not expect

— for we see no one with whom we are in the

— acquainted, or in whose proceedings we have

— Interest. You must not expect scandal

— by the same rule we are equally debarred

— from hearing or inventing it. — You must

— t from me nothing but the melancholy

— sions of a broken Heart which is ever re:

— ing to the Happiness it once enjoyed and

— ill supports its present Wretchedness.

to speak.

— Possibility of being able to write, to you of

— ost Henry will be a Luxury to me, & your

goodness will not I know refuse to read it
it will so much relieve my Heart to write
once thought that to have what is ingener
called a Friend (I mean one of my own Se
to whom I might speak with less reserve'd
to any other person) independant of my
would never be an object of my wishes, but s
much was I mistaken! Charlotte is too m
engrossed by two confidential Correspondents
that sort, to supply the place of one to me
I hope you will not think me girlishly s
tie, when I say that to have some kind
compassionate Friend who might listen to
sorrows without endeavoring to console m
was what I had for some time wished f
when our acquaintance with you, the in

acy which followed it & the particular affec:
nate attention you paid me almost from
first, caused me to entertain the flattering
of those attentions being improved on a
er acquaintance into a Freindship which
you were what my wishes formed you
to be the greatest Happiness I could be
able of enjoying. To find that such Hopes
realized is a satisfaction indeed, a satisfac:
which is now almost the only one I
ever experience. — I feel myself so languid
t I am sure were you with me you would
e me to leave off writing, & I cannot give you
ater proof of my affection for you than by
ing as I know you would wish me to do,
ther Absent or Present. I am my dear Thomas sincere
friend E. L.

Letter the Ninth

Mrs Marlowe to Miss Luttrell

Grosvenor Street, April

Need I say my dear Eloisa how welcom
your letter was to me? I cannot give a c
:er proof of the pleasure I received from it,
of the Desire I feel that our Correspondenc
may be regular & frequent than by setting y
so good an example as I now do in answer
it before the end of the week —. But do not
:give that I claim any merit in being so pu
:tual; on the contrary I assure you, that it is a
greater Gratification to me to write to you, than
spend the Evening either at a Concert or a
Mr Marlowe is so desirous of my appear
at some of the Public places every evenin
I do not like to refuse him, but at the s

so much wish to remain at Home, that in:
ndant of the Pleasure I experience in devoting
portion of my Time to my Dear Eloisa, yet the
ty I claim from having a Letter to write of
ding an Evening at home with my little
You know me well enough to be sensible
of itself be a sufficient Inducement (if one
cessary) to my maintaining with Pleasure
respondence with you. As to the Subjects of
Letters to me, whether Grave or Merry, if
concern you they must be equally interesting
one; Not but that I think the Melancholy
dgence of your own Sorrows by repeating them
elling on them to me, will only encourage
increase them, and that it will be more
ent in you to avoid so sad a subject; but

yet knowing as I do what a soothing & melancholy Pleasure it must afford you, I cannot prevail on myself to deny you so great an Indulgence; and will only insist on your not expecting me to encourage you in it, by my own Letters; on the contrary I intend to fill with such lively Wit and enlivening Hum as shall even provoke a Smile in the sad but sorrowfull countenance of my Eloisa.

In the first place you are to learn that have met your Sisters three friends Lady and her Daughters, twice in Public since have been here. I know you will be impa to hear my opinion of the Beauty of those of whom you have heard so much. Now, as are too ill & too unhappy to be vain, I th I may venture to inform you that I li

…e of their faces so well as I do your own. Yet

…are all handsome – Lady Lesley indeed I have

…before; her Daughters I believe would in

…ral be said to have a finer face than her

…ship, and yet what with the charms of

…blooming Complexion, a little Affectation

…a great deal of Small-talk, (in each of

…ch she is superior to the young Ladies) she

…I dare say gain herself as many admirers

…the more regular features of Matilda, &

…rgaret. I am sure ~~that~~ you will agree with

…in saying that they can none of them be

…proper size for real Beauty, when you

…w that two of them are taller & the other

…er than ourselves. In spite of this Defect

…rather by reason of it) there is something

very noble & majestic in the figures of the
Miss Lesleys, and something agreably lively
in the appearance of their pretty little Ma
-in-law. But tho' one may bee majestic & the
other lively, yet the faces of neither possess
that Bewitching Sweetness of my Eloisas, who
her present Languor is so far from dimin
-ing. What would my Husband and Brother
say of us, if they knew all the fine things I
have been saying to you in this Letter. It's
very hard that a pretty Woman is never to
be told she is so by any one of her own Sex, with
:out that person's beeing suspected to be eith
her determined Enemy, or her professed Toad
How much more amiable are women in th
particular! one Man may say forty civil thing

...ther without our supposing that he is
...paid for it, and provided he does his
...ty by our Sex, we care not how Polite he
...to his own.

M.rs Luttrell will be so good as to accept
...est Complements, Charlotte, my Love,
...Eloisa the best wishes for the recovery
...eir Health & Spirits that can be offered
...er affectionate Friend E. Marlowe.

I am afraid ~~that~~ this Letter will be
...a poor Specimen of my Powers in the
...g Way; and your opinion of them will
...be greatly increased when I assure you
...t I have ~~not~~ been as entertaining as I
...bly could ——.

Letter the Tenth

From Miss Margaret Lesley to Miss Charlotte Lutt[...]

Portman Square. April 13[...]

My dear Charlotte

We left Lesley - Castle on the 28th o[...]
last Month, and arrived safely in London af[...]
a Journey of seven Days; I had the pleasure[...]
of finding your Letter here waiting my Arriva[...]
for which you have my grateful Thanks. A[...]
my dear Freind I every day more regret the
serene & tranquil Pleasures of the Castle we
left, in exchange for the uncertain & unequa[...]
amusements of this vaunted City. Not Th[...]
I will pretend to assert that these uncer[...]
and unequal Amusements are in the l[...]

...ee unpleasing to me; on the contrary I enjoy

...n extremely and should enjoy them even

..., were I not certain that every appear-

...e I make in Public but rivetts the

...ins of those unhappy Beings whose

...sion it is impossible not to pity, tho'

...is out of my power to return. In short

...Dear Charlotte it is my sensibility for

... sufferings of so many amiable young

..., my Dislike of the extreme admiration

...et with, and my aversion to being so

...brated both in Public, in Private, in Papers,

...Printshops, that are the reasons I cannot

...fully enjoy, the amusements so various

...pleasing of London. How often have I

wished that I possessed as little personal Bea[uty]
as you do; that my figure were as inelega[nt]
my face as unlovely; and my appearance [as]
unpleasing as yours! But ah! what little
chance is there of so desirable an Event;
have had the Small-pox, and must there[fore]
submit to my unhappy fate.

I am now going to intrust you m[y]
dear Charlotte with a secret which ha[s]
long disturbed the tranquillity of my days,
which is of a kind to require the most
:violable Secrecy from you. ~~a~~ Last Monda[y]
~~night~~
~~sennight~~ Matilda & I accompanied Lady L[e]
to a Rout at the Honourable Mrs Kicka[m]
we were escorted by Mr Fitzgerald who is

amiable Young Man in the main, tho'
perhaps a little singular in his Taste — He
is in love with Matilda —. We had scarcely
paid our Complements to the Lady of the House
and curtsied to half a score different people
when my Attention was attracted by the ap:
pearance of a Young Man the most lovely of
his Sex, who at that Moment entered the Room
with another Gentleman & Lady. From the
first moment I beheld him, I was certain that
on him depended the future Happiness of my
Life. Imagine my surprise when he was
introduced to me by the name of Cleveland —
I instantly recognized him as the Brother of

Mrs Marlowe, and the acquaintance of

Charlotte at Bristol. Mr and Mrs M.

the gentleman & Lady who accompanied

(You do not think Mrs Marlowe handsome?)

elegant address of Mr Cleveland, his polished Ma

and Delightful Bow, at once confirmed my att

-ment. He did not speak; but I can imagine ev

thing he would have said, had he opened his

I can picture to myself the cultivated Underst

-ing, the Noble Sentiments, & elegant Language

would have shone so conspicuous in the conver

of Mr Cleveland. The approach of Sir James Go

(one of my too numerous admirers) preve

the Discovery of any such Powers, by putt

                                                                            never

an end to a Conversation we had ~ common

and by attracting my attention to himself

—Oh! how inferior are the accomplishments
Sir James to those of his so greatly envied Rivals.
James is one of the most ^frequent of our ~~most~~
...tors. & is almost always of our Parties.
have since often met Mr & Mrs Marlowe
...no Cleveland — he is always engaged some
...e else. Mrs Marlowe fatigues me to Death
...y time I see her by her tiresome conversa:
...s about You & Eloisa. She is so Stupid!
...ve in the hope of seeing her intolerable
...ther to night, as we are going to Lady
...mbeau's, who is I know intimate with the
...lowes. Her party will be Lady Lesley, Ma:
..., Fitzgerald, Sir James Gower, & myself. We see
...of Sir George, who is almost always at the

Gaming-table. Ah! my poor Fortune where
thou by this time? We see more of Lady
who always makes her appearance (highly
-ed) at Dinner-time. Alas! what Delightful
Jewels will she be decked in this evening
Lady Flambeau's; yet I wonder how she can
-self delight in wearing them; surely she
must be sensible of the ridiculous impropriety
loading her little diminutive figure with so
superfluous ornaments; is it possible that she
not know how greatly superior an elegant
simplicity is to the most studied apparel.
Would she but present them to Matilda & me
greatly should we be obliged to her. How becom
would Diamonds be on our finer majestic figur

how surprising it is that such an Idea
should never have occurred to her. I am sure
have reflected in this manner once, I
fifty times. Whenever I see Lady Lesley
ed in them such reflections immediately
across one. My own Mother's Jewels too!
I will say no more on so melancholy
ject — Let me entertain you with some-
ing more pleasing — Matilda had a letter
Morning from Lesley, by which we have
pleasure of finding that he is at Naples
turned Roman-catholic, obtained one
he Pope's Bulls for annulling his 1st Marriage
has since actually married a Neapolitan
of great Rank & Fortune. He tells us more
                                                    -over-

that much the same sort of affair has be[en]

his first wife the worthless Louisa who i[s]
turned Roman-
likewise at Naples has ~~obtained anoth[er]~~
-lic. and is soon to be married
~~the Pope's Bulls for annulling~~ to a Neap[o]
-tan Nobleman of great & Distinguished [?]

He says, that they are at present very g[ood]

Friends, have quite forgiven all past err[ors]

and intend in future to be very good Ne[igh]

-bours. He invites Matilda & me to pay

a visit in Italy and to bring him his litt[le]

Louisa whom both her Mother, Step-Moth[er?]

and himself are equally desirous of beho[lding]

As to our accepting his invitation, it is at

present very uncertain; Lady Lesley adv[ises]

us to go without loss of time; Fitzgerald [?]

escote us there, but Matilda has some

bts of the Propriety of such a scheme - she

s me to it would be very agreable. I am

ain she likes the Fellow. My Father desires

not to be in a hurry, as perhaps if we

it a few months both he & Lady Lesley will

themselves the pleasure of attending us.

y Lesley says no, that nothing will ever

pt her to forego the amusements of

ighthelmstone for a Journey to Italy merely

e our Brother. "No (says the disagreable

man) I have once in my Life been fool

ugh to travel I dont know how many hun-

d Miles to see two of the Family, and I

d it did not answer, so Deuce take me,

er I am so foolish again." so says her

152

Ladyship, but Sir George still perseveres
saying that perhaps in a Month or two,
may accompany us.

Adieu my Dear Charlotte —

Yr faithful Margaret Leslie

The History of England

from the reign of

Henry the 4.th

to the death of

Charles the 1.st

By a partial, prejudiced, & ignorant Historian.

To Miss Austen eldest daughter of the Rev.d
George Austen, this work is inscribed with
all due respect by

The Author

N.B. There will be very few Dates in
this History.

Henry the 4th

Henry the 4th ascended the throne of E-
-gland much to his own satisfaction in
the year 1399, after having prevailed on his
cousin & predecessor Richard the 2d, to resign
to him, & to retire for the rest of his life
to Pomfret Castle, where he happened to be mur-
-dered. It is to be supposed that Henry was
married, since he had certainly four sons,
it is not in my power to inform the Reader
who was his wife. Be this as it may, he

live for ever, but falling ill, his son the Prince
 Wales came and took away the crown; whereupon
King made a long speech, for which I must
 the Reader to Shakespear's Plays, & the
ince made a still longer. Things being thus
led between them the King died, & was
ded by his son Henry who had previously
 Sir William Gascoigne.

Henry the 5.th

Henry the 5th

CE Austen pin:

 Prince after he succeeded to the throne

grew quite reformed & Amiable, forsak
all his dissipated Companions, & never s
-ing Sir William again. During his reign,
Cobham was burnt alive, but I forget
for. His Majesty then turned his thoughts
France, where he went & fought the fam
Battle of Azincourt. He afterwards married the
daughter Catherine, a very agreable Woman
Shakespear's account. Inspite of all this
-ever he died, and was succeeded by his
Henry.

Henry the 6.th

Henry the 6th

C R Austen fecit

...nnot say much for this Monarch's Sense—
...would I if I could, for he was a Lancastrian.
...ppose you know all about the Wars be-
...en him & the Duke of York who was of the
...t side; if you do not, you had better read
...other History, for I shall not be very diffuse
...this, meaning by it only to vent my
...a against, & shew my Hatred to all those
...le whose parties or principles do not suit
...mine, & not to give information. This
...ig married Margaret of Anjou, a Woman
...se distresses & Misfortunes were so great
...almost to make me who hate her, pity her.
...as in this reign that Joan of Arc lived
...ade such a row among the English. They
...d not have burnt her — but they did. There
...several Battles between the Yorkists &

Lancastrians, in which the former (as they
usually conquered. At length they were overcome; The King was murdered – The
Queen was sent home – & Edward the
Ascended the Throne.

Edward the 4th

Ed: the 4th

This Monarch was famous only for his
Beauty & his Courage, of which the Picture
we have here given of him, & his undaunted
Behaviour in marrying one Woman while
he was engaged to another, are suffi=ent

fs. His Wife was Elizabeth Woodville, a Widow poor Woman, was afterwards confined in ----- by that Monster of Iniquity & Avarice --- the 7th. one of Edward's Mistresses --- Jane Shore, who has had a play written on her, but it is a tragedy & therefore not --- reading. Having performed all these --- actions, his Majesty died, & was succeeded --- his Son.

Edward the 5th

--- unfortunate Prince lived so little --- while that no body had time to draw his --- ture. He was murdered by his Uncle's --- trivance, whose name was Richard the 3.

Richard the 3

Rich the 3
C. C. Austin pinxt

The Character of this Prince has been in
general very severely treated by Historians
but as he was a York, I am rather inclined
to suppose him a very respectable Man. It
has indeed been confidently asserted that he
killed his two Nephews & his Wife, but it
has also been declared that he did not
kill his two Nephews, which I am inclined to
beleive true; & if this is the case, it may
also be affirmed that he did not kill
his Wife, for if Perkin Warbeck was really
the Duke of York, why might not Lambert

...nt be the Widow of Richard. Whether in-
...ent or guilty, he did not reign long in peace,
Henry Tudor E. of Richmond as great a villain
...er lived, made a great fuss about getting
...Crown & having killed the King at the battle
...osworth, he succeeded to it.

King the 7th

Henry the 7th

C Catton Pinx:

This Monarch soon after his accession
...ried the Princess Elizabeth of York, by
...its alliance he plainly proved that
...thought his own right inferior to hers,
...he pretended to the contrary. By this

Marriage he had two sons & two daughters
elder of which Daughters was married to the
of Scotland & had the happiness of being gr
-mother to one of the first Characters in t
World. But of her, I shall have occasion to
more at large in future. The Youngest, w
married first the King of France & secondly
D. of Suffolk, by whom she had one dau
afterwards the Mother of Lady Jane Gr
who tho' inferior to her lovely Cousin
Queen of Scots, was yet an amiable you
Woman & famous for reading Greek whe
other people were hunting. It was in
reign of Henry the 7th that Perkin Wa
& Lambert Simnel before mentioned
their appearance, the former of which
set in the Stocks, took shelter in Bea
Abbey, & was beheaded with the Earl

nwich; & the latter was taken into the
g's kitchen. His Majesty died & was suc:
ded by his son Henry whose only merit
· his not being quite so bad as his g——
ghter Elizabeth.

Henry the 8th ————

would the son

It would be an affront to my Readers
& I to suppose that they were not as
· acquainted with the particulars of this
g's reign as I am myself. It will there
be saving them the task of reading again
t they have read before, & myself the

trouble of writing what I do not perfect[ly]
recollect, by giving only a slight sketch of
principal Events which marked his re[ign?]
Among these may be ranked Cardinal
-sey's telling the father Abbott of Leicas
Abbey that "he was come to lay his b[ones?]
among them," the reformation in Reli[gion]
& the King's riding through the streets [of]
London with Anna Bullen. It is however
Justice, & my Duty to declare that this a[miable?]
-able Woman was entirely innocent of [the]
Crimes, with which she was accused ——, of which
Beauty, her Elegance, & her Sprightliness
sufficient proofs, not to mention her so[lemn]
protestations of Innocence, the weakness
the Charges against her, & the King's Cha[racter]
                                                    — ter

of which add some confirmation, tho' perhaps
slight ones when in comparison with
se alledged in her favour. Tho' I do not
~~before~~
... giving many dates, yet as I think
proper to give some & shall of course
... choice of those which it is most ne-
...sary for the Reader to know, I think it
... to inform him that her letter to
... King was dated on the 6.th of May.
Crimes & Cruelties of this Prince, were
numerous to be mentioned, (as this his
I trust has fully shewn) & nothing
be said in his vindication, but that
abolishing Religious Houses & leaving
... to the ruinous depredations of time
... of infinite use to the landscape

of England in general, which probably
was a principal motive for his doing
since otherwise why should a Man who
of no Religion himself be at so much
trouble to abolish one which had for
been established in the Kingdom. His M
5th wife was the Duke of Norfolk's Ne
who, tho' universally acquitted of the
for which she was beheaded, has been
by many people supposed to have
an abandoned life before her Marria
of this however I have many doubt
since she was a relation of that no
Duke of Norfolk who was so warm
the Queen of Scotland's cause, & who a
last fell a victim to it. The King's la

he contrived to survive him, but with diffi-
lty effected it. He was succeeded by his
ly son Edward.

Edward the 6th

Ed: 6th
C E Austen pinxit

As this prince was only nine
...rs old at the time of his Father's
...th, he was considered by many
...ple as too young to govern, & the late
...g happening to be of the same opinion,
...mother's Brother the Duke of Somerset
... chosen Protector of the realm during

his minority. This Man was on the who[le]
a very amiable Character, & is somewha[t]
of a favourite with me, tho' I would by n[o]
means pretend to affirm that he was eq[ual]
to those first of Men Robert Earl of Essex,
Lamere, or Gilpin. He was beheaded, of w[hich]
he might with reason have been prou[d had]
he known that such was the death of S[cots]
Queen of Scotland; but as it was impossi[ble]
that he should be conscious of what h[ad]
never happened, it does not appear th[at]
he felt particularly delighted with the
-ure of ~~it.~~ After his decease the
Duke of Northumberland had the care o[f the]
King & the Kingdom, & performed his tru[st]
of both: so well that the King died & [the]
Kingdom was left to his daughter in la[w]

Lady Jane Grey, who has been already mentioned as reading Greek. Whether she really understood that language or whether such a study
proceeded only from an excess of ~~Cockyloron~~ vanity
which I believe she was always rather
remarkable, is uncertain. Whatever might
the cause, she preserved the same appearance of knowledge, & contempt of what
generally esteemed pleasure, during the
le of her Life; for she declared herself
pleased with being appointed Queen, and
le conducting to the Scaffold, she wrote
sentence in latin & another in Greek
seeing the dead Body of her Husband
dentally passing that way.

Mary

Mary

C E Austin pinx

This woman had the good luck of

advanced to the throne of England, inspir

of the superior pretensions, Merit & Beau

of her Cousins Mary Queen of Scotland & Jer

Grey. Nor can I pity the Kingdom fo

the misfortunes they experienced dur

her Reign, since they fully deserved the

for having allowed her to succeed her Bro

which was a double piece of folly, since

might have foreseen that as she died wit

Children, she would be succeeded by Mar

isgrace to humanity, that pest of society, Eliza-
th. Many were the people who fell Martyrs
the protestant Religion during her reign;
uppose not fewer than a dozen. She mar-
d Philip King of Spain who in her Sister's
for famous for building Armadas. She died
out issue, & then the dreadful moment came
which the destroyer of all comfort, the deceitful
ayer of trust reposed in her, & the Murdress of
ousin succeeded to the Throne. —

      Elizabeth ———

Elizabeth.

Mary Q. of Scotts.

C. E. Austen pinxt

It was the peculiar misfortune
this Woman to have bad Ministers—
since wicked as she herself was, she cou
not have committed such extensive mis
: chief, had not these vile & abandone
Men connived at, & encouraged her in he
Crimes. I know that it has by many,
ple been asserted & believed that Lord Dar
Sir Francis Walsingham, & the rest of the
who filled the chief Offices of State wer
deserving, experienced, & able Ministers
But Oh! how blinded such Writers & su.
Readers must be to true Merit, to Men
despised, neglected & defamed, if they co
persist in such opinions when they u,
that these Men, these boasted Men w

h Scandals to their Country & their Sea as to
w & assist their Queen in confining for the
ce of nineteen Years, a woman who if the
claims of Relationship & Merit were of no
il, yet as a Queen & as one who condescend
ace confidence in her, had every reason to
t Assistance & protection; and at length
llowing Elizabeth to bring this amiable
an to an untimely, unmerited, and scan-
lous Death. Can any one if he reflects
t for a moment on this blot, this ever-
sting blot upon their Understanding
eir Character, allow any praise to Lord
leigh or Sir Francis Walsingham? Oh! what
st this bewitching Princess whose only
nd was then the Duke of Norfolk, and

whose only ones are now Mrs Whitaker

Mrs Lefroy, Mrs Knight & myself, who in

abandoned by her son, confined by her lord

Abused, reproached & vilified by all, what

must not her most noble Mind have su

=ffed when informed that Elizabeth

had given orders for her Death? Yet she

bore it with a most unshaken fortit

firm in her Mind; Constant in her

-ligion; & prepared herself to meet th

cruel fate to which she was doome

with a magnanimity that could alon

proceed from conscious Innocence. A

Yet could you Reader have believed

possible that some hardened & zealou

Protestants have even abused her for th

dfastness in the Catholic Religion which
flected on her so much credit? But this
striking proof of their narrow souls
rejudiced Judgements who accuse her.
he was executed in the Great Hall at
thering ay Castle (sacred Place!) on Wednesday
8th of February – 1586 —— to the everlasting
roach of Elizabeth, her Ministers, and of
land in general. It may not be unne-
sary before I entirely conclude my account
his ill-fated Queen, to observe that she
been accused of several crimes during
time of her reigning in Scotland, of
h I now most seriously do assure my
der that she was entirely innocent; ha-
s never been guilty of anything more

than Imprudencies into which she wa
betrayed by the openness of her Heart, he
Youth, & her Education. Having I trust
this assurance entirely done away eve
Suspicion & every doubt which might ha
arisen in the Reader's mind, from wha
other Historians have written of her, I sh
proceed to mention the remaining Eve
that marked Elizabeth's reign. It was a
this time that Sir Francis Drake th
first English Navigator who sailed rou
the World, lived, to be the ornament of
Country & his profession. Yet great as h
was, & justly celebrated as a Sailor, I can
help foreseeing that he will be equalle
in this or the next Century by one who b

t young, already promises to answer all
-ardent & sanguine expectations of his
ations & Friends, amongst whom I may
t the amiable Lady to whom this work
dedicated, & my no less amiable Self.

Though of a different profession, and
ining in a different Sphere of Life,
equally conspicuous in the Character
an Earl, as Drake was in that of a
lor, was Robert Devereux Lord Essex.
is unfortunate young Man was not
like in Character to that equally un-
tunate one Frederic Delamere. The simile
be carried still farther, & Elizabeth the
ent of Essex may be compared to the
meline of Delamere. It would be endless

to recount the misfortunes of this no
& gallant Earl. It is sufficient to say th
he was beheaded on the 25th of Feb:ry, a
having been Lord Lieutenant of Ireland, af
having clapped his hand on his sword,
after performing many other services to
Country. Elizabeth did not long survive
loss, & died so miserable that were it
an injury to the memory of Mary I sh
pity her.

James the 1st

James the 1st

C E Austin pinxit

Though this Being had some faults, among
its & as the most principal, was his
owing his Mother's death, yet considered
the whole I cannot help liking him.
married Anne of Denmark, and had
—al Children; fortunately for him his
—st son Prince Henry died before his father,
he might have experienced the evils which
—ll his unfortunate Brother.

As I am myself partial to the ro-
—an catholic religion, it is with infi:
—t regret that I am obliged to blame the
—aviour of any Member of it; yet Truth
—g I think very excusable in an Historian,
—niecessitated to say that in this reign
—oman Catholics of England did not

behave like Gentlemen to the protestan

Their Behaviour indeed to the Royal Fam

& both Houses of Parliament might jus

be considered by them as very uncivil,

even Sir Henry Percy tho' certainly the be

bred Man of the party, had none of the

general politeness which is so universa

pleasing, as his Attentions were entire

confined to Lord Mounteagle.

Sir Walter Raleigh flourished in this

the preceding reign, & is by many peop

held in great veneration & respect — Bu

he was an enemy of the noble Essex,

have nothing to say in praise of him

must refer all those who may wish to be a

-quainted with the particulars of his Ly

Mr Sheridan's play of the Critic, where they
l find many interesting Anecdotes as
e of him, as of his friend Sir Christopher
Hatton.—His Majesty was of that amiable
sposition which inclines to Friendships, &
such points was possessed of a keener pene-
tion in Discovering Merit than many others
le. I once heard an excellent Sharade on a
ct, of which the subject I am now on
mind me, and as I think it may afford
Readers some Amusement to find it out,
all here take the liberty of presenting
them.

Sharade ——

first is what my second was to bring
s the 1st. and you read on my whole —

The principal favourites of his Majesty
were Car, who was afterwards created E.
of Somerset and whose name perhaps
have some share in the above-mentioned Plot
& George Villiers afterwards Duke of Buckingham
On his Majesty's death he was succeeded
his son Charles.

Charles the 1st

Charles the 1st

C.E. Austen pinxt

This amiable Monarch seems born to have
suffered Misfortunes equal to those of

ly Grandmother; Misfortunes which he could

t deserve since he was her descendant.

er certainly were there before so many

table Characters at one time in England

in this period of its History; Never were

iable Men so scarce. The number of

m throughout the whole Kingdom amounted

only to five, besides the inhabitants

xford who were always loyal to their

g & faithful to his interests. The names

this noble five who never forgot the duty

he Subject, or swerved from their attach-

nt to his Majesty, were as follows—

King himself, ever stedfast in his

support— Archbishop Laud, Earl of

afford, Viscount Faulkland & Duke of Ormond

who were scarcely less strenuous or zeal[ous]
in the cause. While the Villains of th[at]
time would make too long a list to b[e]
written or read; I shall therefore content
myself with mentioning the leaders [of]
the Gang. Cromwell, Fairfax, Hampd[en]
& Pym may be ~~be~~ considered as th[e]
original Causers of all the disturb[ances]
Distresses, & Civil Wars in which Engl[and]
for many years was embroiled. In th[e]
reign as well as in that of Elizabeth, I [am]
obliged in spite of my attachment to th[e]
Scotch, to consider them as equally gu[ilty]
with the generality of the English, sin[ce]
they dared to think differently from th[eir]
Sovereign, to forget the Adoration which [they]

acts it was their Duty to pay them, to
l against, dethrone & imprison the un-
tunate Mary; to oppose, to deceive, and
sell the no less unfortunate Charles.
Events of this Monarch's reign are
numerous for my pen, and indeed
recital of any Events (except what I
uninteresting
be myself) is ~~interesting~~ to me; my prin-
cial reasons for undertaking the History
England being to prove the innocence
the Queen of Scotland, which I flatter my-
lf with having effectually done, and
buse Elizabeth, tho' I am rather fearful
having fallen short in the latter part
y Scheme. — As therefore it is not

186

my intention to give any particular ac
-count of the distresses into which the
Thing was involved through the misc
-duct & Cruelty of his Parliament, I
shall satisfy myself with vindicate
him from the Reproach of Arbitra
& tyrannical Government with whic
he has often been Charged. This, I f
is not difficult to be done, for w
one argument I am certain of satis
every sensible & well disposed pers
whose opinions have been properly
guided by a good Education — & th
argument is that he was a Stuar

Finis   Saturday Nov: 26

To Miss Cooper —

Cousin —

Conscious of the Charming Character
which in every Country, & every Clime in
Christendom is Cried. Concerning you, with
caution & Care I Commend to your Charitable
Criticism this Clever Collection of Curious
Comments. which have been Carefully Culled,
Collected & Classed by your Comical Cousin

The Author.

A Collection of Letters —

Letter the first

From a Mother to her friend.

My Children begin now to claim all my at
:tention in a different Manner ~~to~~ from that in
they have been used to receive it, as the
are now arrived at that age when it
necessary for them in some measure to
-come conversant with the World. My eldg
is 17 & her Sister scarcely a twelvemon
younger. I flatter myself that their educa
has been such as will not disgrace th
appearance in the World, & that they wi
not disgrace their Education I have every
son to believe. Indeed they are sweet G

sible yet unaffected — Accomplished yet
, —. Lively yet Gentle —. As their progress
every thing they have learnt has been
says the same, I am willing to forget
difference of age, and to introduce them
ther into Public. This very Evening is
d on as their first entrée into life, as we
to drink tea with M.rs Cope & her Daughter.
n glad that we are to meet no one for my
ls sake, as it would be awkward for them
ter too wide a Circle on the very first day.
we shall proceed by degrees —. Tomorrow
Stanly's family will drink tea with us, and
                                    ^
aps the Miss Phillips's will meet them.
Tuesday we shall pay Morning-Visits —
Wednesday we are to dine at Westbrook.
Thursday we have Company at home. On
ay we are to be at a private Concert

at Sir John Wynne's – & on Saturday we expect
Miss Dawson to call in the Morning, which
will complete my Daughters Introduction to
Life. How they will bear so much dissipation
I cannot imagine; of their Spirits I have no
fear, I only dread their health.

———————

This mighty affair is now happily over
& my Girls are out. — As the moment approached for our departure, you can have
no idea how the sweet Creatures trembled
with fear & expectation. Before the Carriage
drove to the door, I called them into my
Dressing-room, & as soon as they were
seated thus addressed them. "My dear Girls
the moment is now arrived when I am to
reap the rewards of all my Anxieties &
Labours towards you during your Education.
You are this Evening to enter a World in
which you will meet with many wonders

...igs; yet let me warn you against suffering

...selves to be meanly swayed by the Follies

...ies of others, for believe me my beloved

...ren that if you do —————— I shall be

sorry for it." They both assured me that

...would ever remember my advice

Gratitude, & follow it with Attention;

...t they were prepared to find a World

... of things to amaze & to shock them:

that they trusted their behaviour

...d never give me reason to repent

...watchful care with which I had pre-

...ded over their infancy & formed their

...d —" "With such expectations & such in-

...tions (cried I) I can have nothing to fear

...you — & can chearfully conduct you to

...enes without a fear of your being

~~seduced~~ ^contaminated by^

~~taminated~~ by her Example, or her Follies

..., then my Children (added I) the

Carriage is driving to the door, & I will [in?]
a moment delay the happiness you are
so impatient to enjoy." When we arr[ived]
at Warleigh, poor Augusta could scarce
breathe, while Margaret was all Life &
Rapture. "The long-expected Moment is
arrived (said she) and we shall soon be [in]
the World". — In a few Moments we wer[e]
in Mrs Cope's parlour, where with her [Daugh?]
:ter she sate ready to receive us. I obser[ved]
with delight the impression my Child[ren]
made on them—. They were indeed tw[o]
sweet, elegant-looking Girls, & tho' som[e]
:what abashed from the peculiarity of [their]
Situation, Yet there was an ease in th[eir]
Manners & Address which could not fa[il]
of pleasing—. Imagine my dear Mad[am]
how delighted I must have been in [?]

Being as I did, how attentively they observed
y object they saw, how disgusted with
e things, how enchanted with others, how
ished at all! On the whole however
returned in raptures with the World,
Inhabitants, & Manners.

&c. Ever — A. F. —

s the Second

n a Young Lady crossed in love to her friend ——

—————

Why should this last disappointment
y so heavily on my Spirits? Why should
d it more, why should it wound me
er than those I have experienced before?
it be that I have a greater affection for
ughtly than I had for his amiable pre:
ssors? Or is it that our feelings become
acute from being often wounded? I

must suppose my dear Belle that this
the case, since I am not conscious of
more sincerely attached to Willoughby tha
I was to Neville, Fitzowen, or either of th
Crawfords, for all of whom I once felt
most lasting affection that ever warme
a Woman's heart. Tell me then dear
why I still sigh when I think of the fa
-less Edward, or why I weep when I be
his Bride? for too surely this is the case—
Friends are all alarmed for me; They fea
my declining health; they lament my u
of Spirits; they dread the effects of both
In hopes of relieving my Melancholy,
directing my thoughts to other objects,
have invited several of their friends
spend the Christmas with us. Lady Bridg
-wood & her Sister in law Miss Jane are
-pected on Friday; & Colonel Seaton's family

...ith us next week. This is all most

...dly meant by my Uncle & Cousins; but

...t can the presence of a dozen indifferent

...le do to me, but weary & distress me —.

...le not finish my Letter tile some of

...Visitors are arrived.

———————

Friday Evening —

...ady Bridget came this Morning, and with

...her sweet Sister Miss Jane —. Although

...ve been acquainted with this charming

...an above fifteen Years, Yet I never before

...ued how lovely she is. She is now a:

...t 35, & in spite of sickness, Sorrow and

...e is more blooming than I ever saw a

...of 17. I was delighted with her, the

...ent she entered the house, & she ap:

...ed equally pleased with me, attaching

...lf to me during the remainder of the

day. There is something so sweet, so m[...]
in her Countenance, that she seems [...]
than Mortal. Her Conversation is as bea[...]
:ing as her appearance; I could not h[...]
telling her how much she engaged m[...]
admiration.. "Oh! Miss Jane (said I) — a[...]
stopped from an inability at the mom[...]
of expressing myself as I could wish — "[...]
Miss Jane — (I repeated) — I could not th[...]
of words to suit my feelings.. She seem[...]
waiting for my Speech —. I was confused —
-fused — My thoughts were bewildered —
I could only add — "How do you do?" She s[...]
& felt for my Embarrassment & with adm[...]
:rable presence of mind relieved me,
it by saying — "My dear Sophia be not[...]
:easy at having exposed Yourself — I wi[...]
turn the Conversation without appeari[...]
to notice it." Oh! how I loved her for her k[...]
:ness! "Do you ride as much as you used t[...]

she.. "I am advised to ride by my Physician,
have delightful Rides round us, I have
charming horse, am uncommonly fond
he Amusement, replied I quite recovered
my Confusion, & in short I ride a great
l." "You are in the right my Love," said she,
repeating the following line which was
atempore & equally adapted to recommend
Riding & Candour —
le where you may, Be Candid where You can,"
added, "I rode once, but it is many years
She spoke this in so low & tremulous a
, that I was silent — Struck with her
ner of speaking I could make no reply.
e not ridden, continued she fixing her
on my face, since I was married."
s never so surprised — "Married, Ma'am!" I
ted.. "You may well wear that look of
ishment, said she, since what I have said

must appear improbable to you – Yet
.thing is more true than that I once
married."

"Then why are you called Miss Jane?"

"I married my Sophia without the con
~~of knowledge~~ of my Father the late Adm.
Annesley. It was therefore necessary to k
the secret from him & from every one, t
some fortunate opportunity might offe
of revealing it –. Such an opportunity
was but too soon given in the death
my dear Capt. Dashwood – Pardon these
continued Miss Jane wiping her Eyes, I o
them to my Husband's memory. He,
my Sophia, while fighting for his Coun
in America after a most happy Unio
seven years–. My Children, two sweet h
e a Girl. who had constantly resided w
my Father & me, passing with him & w

...y one as the Children of a Brother (tho'
... ever been an only Child) had as yet
... the Comforts of my Life. But no sooner
... I lost my Henry, than these sweet
... tures fell sick & died -- . Conceive dear
...lia what my feelings must have been
... as an Aunt I attended my Children
... their earlier Grave --. My Father did not
... vive them many weeks - He died, poor
... old Man, happily ignorant to his last
... r of my Marriage.

... A did not you own it, & assume his
... e at your husband's death.³"

... I could not bring myself to do it; more
...ially when in my Children. I took ale
...cument for doing it. Lady Bridget, and
...self are the only persons who are in the
...oledge of my having ever been either Wife
...ther. As I could not prevail on myself to

take the name of Dashwood (a name wh
after my Henry's death I could never hea
without emotion) and as I was conscious
having no right to that of Annesley, I dr
all thoughts of either, & have made it a point
bearing only my Christian one since my
Father's death." She paused. "Oh! my dea
Miss Jane (said I) how infinitely am I oblig
to you for so entertaining a Story.' You ca
not think how it has diverted me! But
have you quite done?"

"I have only to add my dear Sophia, th
my Henry's elder Brother dieing about th
same time, Lady Bridget became a Wid
like myself, and as we had always l
each other in idea from the high Char
in which we had ever been spoken
though we had never met, we determ
to live together. We wrote to one another
the same subject by the same post, so

our feelings & our actions coincide! We
h eagerly embraced the proposals we gave
ceived of becoming one family, & have
n that time lived together in the great:
affection."

d is this all? said I, I hope you have
done."

deed I have; and did you ever hear a
more pathetic?"

ever did — and it is for that reason it
s me so much, for when one is unhappy
hing is so delightful to one's sensations
to hear of equal misery."

". but my Sophia why are you unhappy?
re you not heard Madam of Willoughby's
iage?" "But my love why lament his
dy, when you bore so well that of many
g Men before?" "Ah! Madam. I was used
them, but when Willoughby broke his
gements I had not been disapointed for
a year." "Poor Girl!" said Miss Jane.

202

Letter the third

From a young Lady in distressed Circumstances to her

―――――――

A few days ago I was at a private Ball
by Mr Ashburnham. As my Mother never g...
out she entrusted me to the care of Lady Gr...
who did me the honour of calling for me i...
her way & of allowing me to sit forwards,
                about
is a favour ~~for~~ which I am very indiffer...
especially as I know it is considered as conf...
a great obligation on me. "To Miss Maria (...
her Ladyship as she saw me advancing t...
door of the Carriage) you seem very sma...
to night – My poor Girls will appear quit...
disadvantage by you – I only hope your Mo...
may not have distressed yourself to set
off. Have you got a new Gown on?"
"Yes Maam." replied I with as much ind...
:fference as I could assume.
"Aye, and a pine one too I think – (feeling

her permission I seated myself by her) I
say it is all very smart – But I must
for you know I always speak my mind,
I think it was quite a needless piece of
nce – Why could not you have worn your old
ned one? It is not my way to find fault
people because they are poor, for
ways think that they are more to be
ised & pitied than blamed for it, especially
hey cannot help it, but at the same
e I must say that in my opinion your
triped Gown would have been quite fine
gh for its wearer – for to tell you the truth
ways speak my mind) I am very much
d that one half of the people in the
will not know whether you have a
on or not – But I suppose you intend
ake your fortune tonight –: Well, the
r the better; & I wish you success."

"Indeed Ma'am I have no such intention" –
"Who ever heard a Young Lady own that she
was a Fortune-hunter?" Miss Greville la[ughed]
but I am sure Ellen felt for me.
"Was your Mother gone to bed before you le[ft]
her?" said her Ladyship.
"Dear Ma'am, said Ellen it is but nine o'cl[ock]
"True – Ellen, but Candles cost money, a[nd]
Mrs Williams is too wise to be extravagant
"She was just sitting down to supper tho'
"And what had she got for Supper?" "I di[d not]
observe." "Bread & Cheese I suppose." "I sho[uld]
never wish for a better supper: said Ellen
"You have never any reason replied her M[o]
: ther, as a better is always provided for y[ou]
Miss Greville laughed excessively, as she con[stant]
: ly does at her Mother's wit.

h is the humiliating Situation in which I am
to appear while riding in her Ladyship's Coach—
not be impertinent, as my Mother is
ays admonishing one to be humble & patient
wish to make my way in the world. She
ists on my accepting every invitation of
Guville, or you may be certain that I would
enter either her House, or her Coach
the disagreeable certainty I always have
eing abused for my Poverty while I am in
. — When we arrived at Ashburnham, it
nearly ten o'clock, which was an hour
a half later than we were desired to be
; but Lady Guville is too fashionable (or
us herself to be so) to be punctual. The
ing however was not begun as they waited
ifs Guville. I had not been long in the room
I was engaged to dance by Mr Bernard,
just as we were going to stand up, he

recollected that his Servant had got his
Gloves, & immediately ran out to fetch them
In the mean time the Dancing began
& Lady Greville in passing to another
went exactly before me — She saw me
& instantly stopping, said to me tho'
there were several people close to us,
"Hey day, Miss Maria! What cannot you get
a partner? Poor Young Lady! I am afraid your
new Gown was put on for nothing. But don't
despair; perhaps you may get a hop before
the Evening is over." So saying, she passed
without hearing my repeated assurance of
being engaged, & leaving me very much
provoked at being so exposed before every one
Mr Bernard however soon returned & by coming
to me the moment he entered the room, &
leading me to the Dancers my Character I hope
was cleared from the imputation Lady Gre

thrown on it, in the eyes of all the old
is who had heard her speech. I soon forgot
my vexations in the pleasure of dancing
of the most agreable partner in the room.
he is moreover heir to a very large Estate
to see that Lady Greville did not look very
pleased when she found who had been
Choice – She was determined to mortify one,
accordingly when we were sitting down
ween the dances, she came to me with
than her usual insulting importance
nded by Miss Mason – and said loud enough
e heard by half the people in the room,
as Miss Maria in what way of business
your Grandfather? for Miss Mason & I cannot
e whether he was a Grocer or a Bookbinder."
o that she wanted to mortify me, and was
ased if I possibly could to prevent her seeing
her scheme succeeded. "Neither Madam; he

was a Wine Merchant." "Aye, I knew he was
in some such low way — He broke did no
"I believe not Ma'am." "Did not he abscond
"I never heard that he did." "At least he died
insolvent?" "I was never told so before." "Was
not your Father as poor as a Rat?" "I am
not, but ~~you probably him knew that~~" "Was
he in the Kings Bench once?" ~~I heard~~
~~body~~ "I never saw him there." "She
gave me such a look, & turned away in
great passion; while I was half delighted
with myself for my impertinence, & half
afraid of ~~being~~ being thought too saucy.
As Lady Greville was extremely angry with
me, she took no further notice of me all the
Evening, and indeed had I been in favour
I should have been equally neglected, as she
got into a party of great folks & she never
speaks to me when she can to any one of

/ Greville was with her Mother's party at
ner, but **Ellen** preferred staying with
Bernards & me. We had a very pleasant
ce & as Lady G— slept all the way home,
d a very comfortable ride.

he next day while we were at dinner
Greville's Coach stopped at the door, for
is the hour of day she generally com:
is it should. She sent in a message by
servant to say "that she should not get
but that Miss Maria must come to the
h-door, as she wanted to speak to her, and
t she must make haste & come imme:
itely —" "What an impertinent Message
na!" said I — "Go Maria—" replied She —
rdingly I went & was obliged to stand
e at her Ladyship's pleasure though the
d was extremely high and very cold.

"Why I think Miss Maria you are not quite
so smart as you were last night – But I [do]
not come to examine your dress, but to [tell]
you that you may dine with us the day
[af]ter tomorrow – Not tomorrow, remember,
not come tomorrow, for we expect Lord and [Lady]
Clermont & Sir Thomas Stanley's family –
There will be no occasion for your being
fine for I shant send the Carriage – If it
rains you may take an umbrella–" I
hardly help laughing at hearing her g[ive]
me leave to keep myself dry – "And pr[ay]
remember to be in time, for I shant wa[it]
I hate my Victuals over-done – But you [are]
not come before the time – How does your M[other]
do? She is at dinner is not she?" "Y[es]
Ma'am we were in the middle of dinn[er]
when your Ladyship came." "I am afrai[d]
you find it very cold Maria." said Elle[n]

s, it is an horrible East wind—said her
ther—I assure you I can hardly bear the
door down—But you are used to be blown
at by the wind Miss Maria & that is
it has made your complexion so rudely
arse. You young Ladies who cannot often
in a Carriage never mind what wea:
r you trudge in, or how the wind shews your
s I would not have my Girls stand
of doors as you do in such a day as this.
t ~~you~~ some sorts, of people have no feelings
er of cold or Delicacy—Well, remember
t we shall expect you on Thursday at
ock—You must tell your Maid to come
ou at night—There will be no Moon—
You will have an horrid walk home—
Comp^ts to your Mother—I am afraid
r dinner will be cold—Drive on—
away she went, leaving me in a
t passion with her as she always does.
                              Maria Williams

Letter the fourth

From a young Lady rather impertinent to her f

—————

We dined yesterday with Mr Evelyn where
were introduced to a very agreable looking
his Cousin. I was extremely pleased with
appearance, for added to the charms of
engaging face, her manner & voice had som
: thing peculiarly interesting in them. So
so, that they inspired me with a great cu
: ty to know the history of her Life, who
her Parents, where she came from, and wh
had befallen her, for it was then only know
that she was a relation of Mr Evelyn,
that her name was Grenville. In the &
a favourable opportunity offered to me of a
: tempting at least to know what I wished
know, for every one played at Cards but M.
Evelyn, My Mother, Dr Drayton, Miss Grenville.

...self, and as the two former were engaged in
...hispering Conversation, & the Doctor fell
...eep, we were of necessity obliged to en:
...tain each other. This was what I wished
... being determined not to remain in
...rance for want of asking, I began the
...versation in the following Manner.

..."ave you been long in Essex ma'am?"
..."...rived on Tuesday."

..."...came from Derbyshire?"

..."...ma'am—! appearing surprised at my
...stion, from Suffolk." "You will think
...a good dash of mine my dear Mary,
...you know that I am not wanting
...Impudence when I have any end in view
...e you pleased with the Country Miss Gran-
...lle? Do you find it equal to the one you
...ve left?"

"Much superior Ma'am in point of Beau

She sighed. I longed to know for why.

"But the face of any Country however

beautiful said I. can be but a poor cons

:lation for the loss of one's dearest Frie

She shook her head, as if she felt the tru

of what I said. My Curiosity was so m

raised, that I was resolved at any ra

to satisfy it.

"You regret having left Suffolk then My

Grenville?"   "Indeed I do."   "You we

born there I suppose?"   "Yes Ma'am I w

b passed many happy years there —

"That is a great comfort — said I. I hop

Ma'am that you never spent any u

= happy ones there."

"Perfect Felicity is not the property of M

...ls, & no one has a right to expect un-

Happiness.

-rupted ~~Felicity~~ — Some Misfortunes

we certainly meet with —"

...t Misfortunes dear Ma'am? replied

...ning with impatience to know every

...g. "None Ma'am I hope that have

...the effect of any wilfull fault in ma...

...re say not Ma'am; & have no doubt

that any sufferings you may have

...rinced could ~~arise~~ arise only from the cru-

...s of Relations or the Errors of Freinds."

...ighed — "You seem unhappy my dear

...Grenville — Is it in my power to sof-

...your Misfortunes?" "Your power

...am ~~replied~~ replied she extremely surprised:

...s in no one's power to make me happy.

...pronounced these words in so mournfull

& solemn an accent, that for some time
had not courage to reply. I was actually
silenced. ⟨~~Do you then believe it then~~⟩
I recovered myself however in a few mo-
:ments & looking at her with all the a-
:tion I could, "My dear Miss Grenville sa
you appear extremely young. I may p
:bably stand in need of some one's ad
whose regard for you, joined to superi
:age, perhaps superior Judgement m
authorise her to give it. I am that p
:son, & I now challenge you to accept
offer I make you of my Confidence a
Friendship, in return to which I sha
only ask for yours."

"You are extremely obliging Ma'am
said She. & I am highly flattered by yo
attention to me. But I am in no d
:ficulty, no doubt, no uncertainty o
:tuation in which any Advice can be w

...wer I am however continued she

...ttering into a complaisant smile, I

...ll know where to apply."

...wed, but felt a good deal mortified by

...a repulse; still however I had not gi:

...up my point. I found that by the ap:

...rance of Sentiment & Friendship nothing

...to be gained & determined therefore to

...w my attacks by Questions & Suppositions

...you intend staying long in this part of

...and Miss Grenville?"

...Ma'am; some time I believe."

...t how will Mr & Mrs Grenville bear your

...ce? ~~during a long stay in France~~"

...y are neither of them alive Ma'am."

...was an answer I did not expect —

...s quite silenced, I never felt so auk:

...d in my Life ——.

Letter the fifth

From a Young Lady very much in love to h[er]
Friend.

_____

My Uncle gets more stingy, my Aun[t]
more particular, & I more in love ever[y]
day. What shall we all be at this rate [by]
the end of the year! I had this mornin[g]
the happiness of receiving the following
:ter from my dear Musgrove.

Sackville St: Jan: 7th

It is a month to day since I first behe[ld]
my lovely Henrietta, & the sacred anni
:sary must & shall be kept in a ma[n]
:ner becoming the day — by writing to [her]
Never shall I forget the moment wh[en]
her Beauties first broke on my sight
No time as you well know can erase [it]
from my Memory. It was at Lady Sc[ott]

...es. Happy Lady Scudamore to live within
..ile of the divine Henrietta! When the
..ly Creature first entered the room, Oh!
..t were my sensations? The sight of you was
.. the sight of a wonderful fine Thing.
..tarted — I gazed at her with admiration
..appeared every moment more Charming,
.. the unfortunate Musgrove became
..ptive to your Charms before I had
.. to look about me. Yes Madam, I had
..happiness of adoring you, an happiness
..which I cannot be too grateful. "What
..d he to himself is Musgrove allowed
..ie for Henrietta? Enviable Mortal! and
.. the prize for her who is the object of
..versal admiration, who is adored by a
..nel, & toasted by a Baronet! — Adorable
..nitta how beautiful you are! I declare
..are quite divine! You are more than

Mortal. You are an Angel. You are Venus
herself. In short Madam you are the prettiest
Girl I ever saw in my Life — & her Beauty
is encreased in her Musgrove's Eyes, by
permitting him to love her & allowing him
to hope. And ah! Angelic Miss Henrietta
Heaven is my witness how ardently I
hope for the death of your villanous Uncle
& his abandoned Wife, since my fair one will
not consent to be mine till their deceas
has placed her in affluence above what
my fortune can procure —. Though it is
improvable Estate —. Cruel Henrietta will
persist in such a resolution. I am at pre-
:sent with my Sister where I mean to
continue till my own house which tho
an excellent one is at present some:
:what out of repair, is ready to rece-
:ive me. Amiable princess of my Heart

—of that Heart which trembles while
 —gns itself your most ardent Admirer
                    & devoted humble Serv.t
                         T. Musgrove

~~I hope to receive an answer to this~~
~~many days have tortured me with~~
~~—neid any letter (such, as—) will be~~
~~—ed—~~.

There is a pattern for a Love-letter Ma:
—a! Did you ever read such a master-
—ce of Writing? Such Sense, such senti:
—nt, such purity of Thought, such flow
—nguage & such unfeigned Love in one
—t? No, never I can answer for it, since
—usgrove is not to be met with by every
—. Oh! how I long to be with him! I
~~—nd to send him the following as an:~~
—r to his Letter to morrow.

—dearest Musgrove ———. Words can not express

how happy your letter made me; I thoug[ht]
I should have cried for Joy. for I love you bett[er]
than any body in the World. I think you
most amiable, & the handsomest man [in]
England, & so to be sure you are. I never [saw]
so sweet a letter in my life. Do write
another just like it, & tell me you are [in]
love with me in every other line. I qu[ite]
die to see you. How shall we manage [to]
see one another? for we are so much in [love]
that we cannot live asunder. Oh! my d[ear]
Musgrove you cannot think how impa[tient]
:ly I wait for the death of my Uncle a[nd]
Aunt — If they will not die soon, I b[elieve]
I shall run mad, for I get more in lo[ve]
with you every day of my life.

How happy your Sister is to enjoy the
pleasure of your Company in her hous[e,]

...w happy every body in London must be
...use you are there. I hope you will be so
...d as to write to me again soon, for I never
... such sweet letters as yours. I am my
...st Musgrove most truly & faithfully
...s for ever & ever Henrietta Halton —

...pe he will like my answer; it is as
... a one as I can write, though nothing
...is; Indeed I had always heard what a
...he was at a Love-letter. I saw him
...know for the first time at Lady Sey:
...mour's — And when I saw her Ladyship
...wards She asked me how I liked her
...sin Musgrove?

..."y upon my word said I, I think he is a
..."y handsome young Man."

..."n glad you think so replied She, for he is
...ractedly in love with you."

"Law! Lady Scudamore said I, how can y
talk so ridiculously?"

"Nay, 'tis very true answered she, I assure
for he was in love with you from the fir
moment he beheld you."

"I wish it may be true said I, for that is
only kind of love I would give a farthi
for— There is some sense in being in l
at first sight."

"Well, I give you joy of your conquest, rep
Lady Scudamore, and I believe it to have
been a very complete one; I am su
it is not a contemptible one, for my Cou
is a charming young fellow, has seen
great deal of the World, & writes the best
love-letters I ever read."

This made me very happy, and I was
: cessively pleased with my conquest. H
: ever I thought it was proper to giv

...self a few Airs — So I said to her —

...is is all very pretty Lady Scudamore,
...you know that we young Ladies who
...Heiresses must not throw ourselves
...ay upon Men who have no fortune at
..."

...dear Miss Halton said she, I am as
...ch convinced of that as you can be, and
...assure you that I should be the last
...on to encourage your marrying anyone
...had not some pretensions to expect
...stune with you. Mr Musgrove is so far
...being poor that he has an estate of
...ral hundreds an year which is capable
...reat Improvement, and an excellent
...se, though at present it is not quite
...pair."

...that is the case replied I, I have nothing

more to say against him, and if as you s[ay]
he is an informed young Man and can w[rite]
a good love-letters, I am sure I have no wa[y]
to find fault with him for admiring one, [but]
perhaps I may not marry him for all tha[t]
Lady Sundamore."

"You are certainly under no obligation t[o]
marry him answered her Ladyship, ex[cept]
that which love himself will dicta[te to]
you, for if I am not greatly mistaken
you are at this very moment unkno[wn]
to yourself, cherishing a most tend[er]
affection for him."

"Law, Lady Sundamore replied I blush[ed]
how can you think of such a thing?"
"Because every look, every word betrays [it]
answered she; Come my dear Henrietta, c[on]
-sider me as a friend, and be sincere with

...t you prefer Mr Musgrove to any man of
acquaintance?"

...y do not ask me such questions Lady
...amore, said I turning away my head,
...t is not fit for me to answer them."

... my Love replied she, now you confirm
...uspicions. But why Henrietta should you
...hamed to own a well-placed Love, or
...refuse to confide in me."

...m not ashamed to own it; said I taking
...age. I do not refuse to confide in you
...ush to say that I do love your cousin
...Musgrove, that I am sincerely attached
...im, for it is no disgrace to love a hand-
...e Man. If he were plain indeed I might
...had reason to be ashamed of a passion
...h must have been mean since the
...t would have been unworthy. But
...such a figure & face, & such beautiful

hair as your Cousin has, why should I be
to own that such superior Merit has m[ade]
an impression on me."

"My sweet Girl (said Lady Scudamore emb[racing]
me with great Affection) what a delica[te]
way of thinking you have in these M[at]-
:ters, and what a quick discernment for [one]
of your years! Oh! how I honour you for su[ch]
Noble Sentiments!"

"Do you Ma'am? said I; You are vastly ob[liging]
But pray Lady Scudamore did your Cousin [him]
:self tell you of his Affection for me? I sh[all]
like him the better if he did, for what [is]
a Lover without a Confidante?"

"Oh! my Love replied she, you were bor[n]
for each other. Every word you say more
deeply convinces me that your Mind[s]
are actuated by the invisible power of [sym]
:pathy, for your opinions and Sentiments [so]

tly coincide. Nay, the colour of your Hair
is very different. Yes my dear Girl, the
despairing Musgrove did reveal to me
story of his Love —. Nor was I surprised at
I know not how it was, but I had a kind of
sentiment that he would be in love with you.
e, but how did he break it to you?"
was not till after Supper. We were sit-
round the fire together talking on indif-
nt Subjects, though to say the truth the
rsation was chiefly on my side for he
thoughtful and silent, when on a sudden
interrupted me in the midst of some-
ing I was saying, by exclaiming in a
t Theatrical tone —

Im in love I feel it now

And Henrietta Halton has undone me —

What a sweet Way replied I, of declaring
Passion! To make such a couple of char-
ing Lines about me! What a pity it is that

they are not in rhime."

"I am very glad you like it answered sh
To be sure ~~Indeed~~ there was a great deal of Taste in
and are you in love with her, Cousin? said
I am very sorry for it. for unexceptionabl
as you are in every respect, with a pretty, &
capable of Great improvement, and are e
:cellent House tho' somewhat out of repa
Yet who can hope to aspire with succes
to the adorable Henrietta who has had
offer from a Colonel & been toasted by a Bar
"That I have" cried I. Lady Scudamore conte
"Ah dear Cousin replied he, I am so well c
:vinced of the little Chance I can have of
:ning her who is adored by thousands, th
I need no assurances of yours to make m
more thoroughly so. Yet surely neither y
or the fair Henrietta herself will deny
the exquisite Gratification of dieing for
of falling a victim to her Charms and u

... dead —continued he ————

...dy Scudamore, said I wiping my eyes, that
... a sweet creature should talk of dieing!"

... an affecting Circumstance indeed, replied
...Scudamore. "When I am dead said he, let
...be carried & lain at her feet, & perhaps
...may not disdain to drop a pitying tear
...my poor remains."

... Lady Scudamore interrupted I, say no more
...his affecting subject. I cannot bear it."

...now I admire the sweet sensibility of
...soul, and as I would not for Worlds wound
...deeply, I will be silent."

..., go on." said I. She did so.

... then added he, Ah! Cousin imagine what
...transports will be when I feel the dear
...ous drops trickle o'er my face! Who
...not die to taste such extacy! And
...n I am interred, may the divine Hen:
...etta bless some happier Youth with her

affection, May he be as tenderly attached to
as the hapless Musgrove & while he crum—
to dust, May they live an example of Fe—
:licity in the Conjugal State.'"

Did you ever hear any thing so pathetic
What a charming wish, to be lain at m—
feet when he was dead! Oh! What an e—
:ed mind he must have to be capable
Such a wish! Lady Scudamore went on.

"Ah! my dear Cousin replied I to him, su
noble behaviour as this, must melt the
heart of any Woman however obdurate
may naturally be; and could the divine
Henrietta but hear your generous wis—
for her happiness, all gentle as is he—
Mind, I have not a doubt but that she wa—
pity your affection & endeavour to return—
"Oh! Cousin answered he, do not endeavour
raise my hopes by such flattering Assura—
No, I cannot hope to please this angel of a—

...an, and the only thing which remains
...e to do, is to die. "True love is ever desponding
...d I, but I my dear Tom will give you
...greater hopes of conquering this fair one's
...t, than I have yet given you, by assuring
...that I watched her with the strictest at-
...tion during the whole day, and could
...ily discover that she cherishes in her bo-
...though unknown to herself, a most ten-
...affection for you."

...r Lady Scudamore cried I, this is more
...I # ever knew!"

...not I say that it was unknown to
...self? I did not, continued I to him, en-
...rage you by saying this at first, that
...rise might under the pleasure Pile
...ater. "No Cousin replied he in a languid
...nothing will convince me that I can have
...d the heart of Henrietta Halton, and if you

234

are deceived yourself, do not attempt decei
me." In short my love it was the work of
some hour for me to persuade the poor
despairing Youth that you had really a
preference for him; but when at last
could no longer deny the force of my
:guments, or discredit what I told him
his transports, his Raptures, his ecstac
are beyond my power to describe."

"Oh! the dear Creature; cried I, how pass
:ately he loves me! But dear lady Scu
:more did you tell him that I was t
:tally dependant on my Uncle & Aunt?"

"Yes, I told him every thing."

"And what did he say."

"He exclaimed with violence agai
Uncles & Aunts; Accused the Laws of E
:gland for allowing them to possess the

...tes when wanted by their Nephews or
...is, and wished he were in the House
...ommons, that he might reform the
...islature, & rectify all its abuses."

...the sweet Man! What a Spirit he has."
...J.

...could not flatter himself he added, that
...adorable Henrietta would condescend for
...sake to resign those Luxuries & that
...endor to which she had been used, and
...pt only in exchange the Comforts and
...ancies which his limited Income could
...d her, even supposing that his house
...i in Readiness to receive her. I told him
...t it could not be expected that she
...d; it would be doing her, an injustice
...uppose her capable of giving up the
...r she now possesses & so nobly uses
...doing such extensive good to the poorer
...t of her fellow Creatures, merely for

the gratification of you and herself.

"To be sure said I, I am very charitable now and then. ~~I was two price their~~ replied. And what did Mr Musgrove say to th

"He ~~said~~ that he was under a melanc Necessity of owning the truth of what I s and that therefore if he should be the to be py Creature destined ~~to~~ the Husband o beautiful Henrietta he must bring hi self to wait, however impatiently, for fortunate day, when she might be fre from the power of worthless Relations a able to bestow herself on him."

What a noble Creature he is! Oh! Ma what a fortunate one I am, who am his Wife! My aunt is calling me to co I make the pies. So adieu my dearf I believe one yours &c — H. Ha

Finis

To Miss Fanny Catherine Austen

My dear Neice

    As I am prevented by the great distance
between Rowling & Steventon from superintending
your Education Myself, the care of which will
probably on that account devolve on your Father
& Mother, I think it is my particular Duty to
prevent your feeling as much as possible the want
of my personal instructions, by addressing to You
on paper my Opinions & Admonitions on the conduct
of Young Women, which you will find expressed
in the following pages. — I am my dear Neice

        Your affectionate Aunt

          The Author

The female philosopher —

a Letter.

My dear Louisa

Your friend Mr Millar called upon
yesterday in his way to Bath, whither he is
for his health; two of his daughters were wit
him, but the oldest & the three Boys are with
Mother in Sussex. Though you have often told
that Miss Millar was remarkably handsom
you never mentioned anything of her Sisters
ty; yet they are certainly extremely prett
I'le give you their description. — Julia is
:een; with a countenance in which Modesty
Sense & Dignity are happily blended, she
a form which at once presents you with
Elegance & Symmetry. Charlotte who is just e
:teen is shorter than her Sister, and though
her figure cannot boast the easy dignity

...is, yet it has a pleasing plumpness which
estimable.
a different way as pleasing. She is fair &
...e is expressive sometimes of softness the most
...tching, and at others of Vivacity the most
...ing. She appears to have infinite wit and a
...humour unalterable; her conversation during
...half hour they sat with us, was replete with
...rous Sallies, Bonmots & repartees; while the
...ble, the amiable Julia uttered sentiments
...mity worthy of a heart like her own.
...Millar appeared to answer the character
...d always received of him. My Father met
...with that look of Love, that social Shake,
...dial Kiss which marked his gladness at
...ing an old & valued friend from whom
...various circumstances he had been separat...
...early twenty years. Mr Millar observed
...very justly too) that many events had
...ken place during that interval of time, which
...e occasion to the lovely Julia for making

most sensible reflections on the many chan
in their situation which so long a period th
occasioned, on the advantages of some, & the d
: vantages of others. From this subject she
a short digression to the instability of hu
pleasures & the uncertainty of their dura
which led her to observe that all earthly
must be imperfect. She was proceeding
illustrate this doctrine by examples from
Lives of great Men when the Carriage
to the Door and the amiable Moralist wit
Father & Sister was obliged to depart, but
without a promise of spending five or si
with us on their return. We of course mention
you, and I assure you that ample Justi
was done to your Merits by all. "Louisa Cl
(said I) is in general a very pleasant Gi
yet sometimes her good humour is clouded
Peevishness, Envy & Spite. She neither w

...standing or ^{is} without some pretensions to Beau...
but these are so very trifling, that the value
...ts on her personal charms, & the adoration
...xpects them to be offered are at once a
...ing example of her vanity, her pride, &
...lly." So said I, & to my opinion every one
...d weight by the concurrence of their own.

Your affec:^{te} Arabella Smythe

The first Act of a Comedy ——

...haracters

...guin

...les

...tilion

...rus of ploughboys

...

...ephon

...

...sia

...istoletta

...stefs

...h

...nd

...hloe

Scene — an Inn —

Enter Hostess, Charlies, Maria, & Cook.

Host:^s to Maria/ If the gentry in the Lion still
      want beds, shew them number 9. —

Maria/ Yes Mistress. —   exit Maria —

Host:^s to Cook/ If their Honours in the Moon
      for the bill of fare, give it them.

Cook/ — I will, I will. —   exit Cook.

Host^s to Charles/ If their Ladyships in the Sun
      their Bell — answer it. —

Charles/ Yes Ma'am. — Exeunt Severally —

    Scene changes to the Moon, & disco
    Popgun & Pistoletta.

Pistol:^{tta}/ Pray papa how far is it to London

Popgun/ My girl, my Darling, my favourite
    my Children, who art the picture of thy,
    Mother who died two months ago, with who
    I am going to Town to marry You Strephon
    to whom I mean to bequeath my whole
    it wants seven Miles.

Scene changes to the Sun —

Enter Chloe & a chorus of ploughboys.

1 Where am I? At Hounslow. — Where go I?
To London — What to do? To be married —
Unto whom? Unto Strephon. Who is he?
2 Youth. — Then I will sing a Song.

Song —

I go to Town
And when I come down,
I shall be married to Stree-phon
And that to me will be fun.

¾ Be fun, be fun, be fun,
And that to me will be fun,

Enter Cook —

½ Here is the bill of fare.

¼ reads½ 2 Ducks, a leg of ⟨w⟩beef, a stinking
partridge, & a tart. — I will have the leg
of beef and the partridge. exit Cook.
And now I will sing another song.

Song —

I am going to have my dinner,
After which I shan't be thinner,

I wish I had here Stephen
For he would carve the partridge if it sho
be a tough one.

Chorus / Tough one, tough one, tough one,
For he would carve the partridge if it
Should be a tough one.

Exit Chloe and Chorus —

Scene changes to the inside of the Lion
Enter Stephen & Postilion

Steph:/ You drove me from Staines to this
place, from whence I mean to go to
to marry Chloe. How much is your du

Post:/ Eighteen pence.

Steph:/ Alas, my friend, I have but a
guinea with which I mean to suppo
myself in Town. But I will pawn to
an undirected Letter that I received of
Chloe.

Post:/ Sir, I accept your offer.

End of the first Act. ___

Letter from a Young Lady, whose feelings
too strong for her Judgement led her into
Errors
mission of ~~commission~~ which her
disapproved. ——

Many have been the cares & vicissitudes
past life, my beloved Ellinor, & the only
lation I feel for their bitterness is that on
examination of my conduct, I am convinced
I have strictly deserved them. I murdered
father at a very early period of my Life,
since murdered my Mother, & I am now
g to murder my Sister. I have changed
eligion so often that at present I have
n idea of any left. I have been a per:
d witness in every public tryal for these
twelve Years, and I have forged my own
. In short there is scarcely a crime that
ve not committed — But I am now going to

reform. Colonel Martin of the Horseguards
paid his Addresses to me, & we are to be m
:ried in a few days. As there is someth
Singular in our Courtship, I will give yo
account of it. Col: Martin is the second So
the late Sir John Martin who died immen
rich, but bequeathing only one hundred tho
pound apiece to his three younger Children
the bulk of his fortune, about eight Million
the present Sir Thomas. Upon his small
:tance the Colonel lived tolerably contente
nearly four months when he took it into
head to determine on getting the whole of
eldest Brother's Estate. A new will was f
& the Colonel produced it in Court — but n
would swear to it's being the right Will
:cept himself, & he had sworn so much th
Nobody believed him. At that moment
happened to be passing by the door of th

was beckoned in by the Judge who told
Colonel that I was a Lady ready to witness
ing for the cause of Justice, & advised him
ply to me. In short the Affair was soon
isted. The Colonel & I swore to it' being
ight, will & Sir Thomas has been obliged
sign all his illgotten Wealth. The Colonel
-atitude waited on me the next day with
ffer of his hand —. I am now going to meet
my Sister.   Yrs Ever, Anna Parker.

A Tour through Wales —
in a Letter from a young Lady —

dear Clara
            I have been so long on the ramble
I have not till now had it in my power
ank you for your Letter —. We left our dear
on last monday month; and proceeded on
tour through Wales; with is a principality

contiguous to England and gives the title to
Prince of Wales. We travelled on horseback in
preference. My Mother rode upon our little
:ney & Fanny & I walked by her side or rather
for my Mother is so fond of riding fast that
She galloped all the way: You may be sure
we were in a fine perspiration when we ca
to our place of resting. Fanny has taken a
many Drawings of the Country, which are ve
beautiful, tho' perhaps not such exact rese
:blances as might be wished, from their .
taken as she ran along. It would astonish y
to see all the Shoes we wore out in our To
We determined to take a good Stock with
& therefore each took a pair of our own be
those we set off in. However we were obl
to have them both, capped & heelpieced at
:marthen, & at last when they were qui
gone, Mama was so kind as to lend us a

e Satin Slippers, of which we each took one

hopped home from Fereford delightfully —

    I am your ever affectionate

        Elizabeth Johnson.

   A Tale.

A gentleman whose family name I

e conceal, bought a small Cottage in Pem=

shire about two years ago. This daring

n was suggested to him by his elder

ter who promised to furnish two rooms

Closet for him, provided he would take

all house near the borders of an extensive

&, and about three Miles from the Sea.

elminus gladly accepted the offer and

inued for some time searching after such

eat when he was one morning agreably

ied from his Suspence by reading this ad=

tisement in a Newspaper.

To be Lett

A neat Cottage on the borders of an extensive
: rest & about three Miles from the Sea. N
ready furnished except two rooms & a Closet.

The delighted Wilhelminus posted away
: mediately to his brother, & shewed him the
advertisement. Robertus congratulated him
sent him in his Carriage to take possess
of the Cottage. After travelling for three days
& six Nights without Stopping, they arriv
at the Forest & following a track which
by it's side down a steep Hill over whic
ten Rivulets meandered, they reached the
: tage in half an hour. Wilhelminus a
: ed, and after knocking for some time with
: out receiving any answer — or hearing an
Stir within, he opened the door which w
fastened only by a Wooden latch & entered a s
room, which he immediately perceived to

of the two that were unfurnished – From thence
…ceeded into a closet equally bare. A pair
…airs that went out of it led him into
…n above, no less destitute, to these apart.
…ts he found composed the whole of the
… . He was by no means displeased
this discovery, as he had the comfort
…flecting that he should not be obliged
…y out any thing on furniture him self –
…eturned immediately to his Brother, who
…him the next day to every shop in
…, & bought what ever was requisite to
…ish the two rooms & the Closet. In a
…days every thing was completed, and
…lminius returned to take possession of
…Cottage. Robertus accompanied him, with
…ady the amiable Cæcilia & her two lovely
… Arabella and Marina to whom Wilhel..
…s was tenderly attached, and a large

number of attendants. — An ordinary Gene
might probably have been embarassed.
endeavouring to accomodate so large a par
but Wilhelmina with admirable presence
of mind gave orders for the immediate
:tion of two noble Tents in an open Spa
in the Forest adjoining to the house. The
Construction was both simple & elegant,
a couple of old blankets, each supported
four Sticks, gave a striking proof of tha
Taste for Architecture & that happy ease
in overcoming difficulties which were
of Wilhelmina's most striking Virtue

Finis

End of the Second Volume

VOLUME THE SECOND

—

Ex dono mei Patris

CONTENTS

Love and Friendship   Page [267]

Lesley Castle   [289]

The History of England   [309]

Collection of Letters   [316]

Scraps   [330]

To Madame La Comtesse
De Feuillide This Novel is inscribed
by Her obliged Humble Servant The Author

Love and Freindship

a novel in a series of Letters.
"Deceived in Freindship & Betrayed in Love"

Letter the First
from Isabel to Laura

How often, in answer to my repeated intreaties that you would give my Daughter a regular detail of the Misfortunes and Adventures of your Life, have you said "No, my freind never will I comply with your request till I may be no longer in Danger of again experiencing such dreadful ones." Surely that time is now at hand. You are this Day 55. If a woman may ever be said to be in safety from the determined Perseverance of disagreable Lovers and the cruel Persecutions of obstinate Fathers, surely it must be at such a time of Life.

ISABEL.

Letter 2nd
Laura to Isabel

Altho' I cannot agree with you in supposing that I shall never again be exposed to Misfortunes as unmerited as those I have already experienced, yet to avoid the imputation of Obstinacy or ill-nature, I will gratify the curiosity of your daughter; and may the fortitude with which I have suffered the many Afflictions of my past Life, prove to her a useful Lesson for the support of those which may befall her in her own.

LAURA

Letter 3rd
Laura to Marianne

As the Daughter of my most intimate freind I think you entitled to that knowledge of my unhappy Story, which your Mother has so often solicited me to give you.

My Father was a native of Ireland & an inhabitant of Wales; My Mother was the natural Daughter of a Scotch Peer by an italian Opera-girl—I was born in Spain & received my Education at a Convent in France.

When I had reached my eighteenth Year I was recalled by my Parents to my paternal roof in Wales. Our mansion was situated in one of the most romantic parts of the Vale of Uske. Tho' my Charms are now considerably softened and somewhat impaired by the Misfortunes I have undergone, I was once beautiful. But lovely as I was the Graces of my Person were the least of my Perfections. Of every accomplishment accustomary to my sex, I was Mistress. When in the Convent, my progress had always exceeded my instructions, my Acquirements had been wonderfull for my Age, and I had shortly surpassed my Masters.

In my Mind, every Virtue that could adorn it was centered; it was the Rendezvous of every good Quality & of every noble sentiment.

A sensibility too tremblingly alive to every affliction of my Freinds, my Acquaintance and particularly to every affliction of my own, was my only fault, if a fault it could be called. Alas! how altered now! Tho' indeed my own misfortunes do not make less impression on me than they ever did, yet now I never feel for those of an other. My accomplishments too, begin to fade—I can neither sing so well nor Dance so gracefully as I once did—and I have entirely forgot the *Minuet Dela Cour.*

Adeiu.

LAURA

Letter 4th
Laura to Marianne

Our neighbourhood was small, for it consisted only of your mother. She may probably have already told you that being left by her Parents in indigent Circumstances she had retired into Wales on eoconomical motives. There it was, our freindship first commenced. Isabel was then one and twenty—Tho' pleasing both in her Person and Manners (between ourselves) she never possessed the hundredth part of my Beauty or Accomplishments. Isabel had seen the World. She had passed 2 Years at one of the first Boarding schools in London; had spent a fortnight in Bath & had supped one night in Southampton.

"Beware my Laura (she would often say) Beware of the insipid Vanities and idle Dissipations of the Metropolis of England; Beware of the unmeaning Luxuries of Bath & of the Stinking fish of Southampton."

"Alas! (exclaimed I) how am I to avoid those evils I shall never be exposed to? What probability is there of my ever tasting the Dissipations of London, the Luxuries of Bath or the stinking Fish of Southampton? I who am doomed to waste my Days of Youth & Beauty in an humble Cottage in the Vale of Uske."

Ah! little did I then think I was ordained so soon to quit that humble Cottage for the Deceitfull Pleasures of the World.

adeiu
LAURA

Letter 5th
Laura to Marianne

One Evening in December as my Father, my Mother and myself, were arranged in social converse round our Fireside, we were on a sudden, greatly astonished, by hearing a violent knocking on the outward Door of our rustic Cot.

My Father started—"What noise is that," (said he.) "It sounds like a loud rapping at the Door"—(replied my Mother.) "it does indeed." (cried I.) "I am of your opinion; (said my Father) it certainly does appear to proceed from some uncommon violence exerted against our unoffending Door." "Yes (exclaimed I) I cannot help thinking it must be somebody who knocks for Admittance."

"That is another point (replied he;) We must not pretend to determine on what motive the person may knock—tho' that someone *does* rap at the Door, I am partly convinced."

Here, a 2d tremendous rap interrupted my Father in his speech and somewhat alarmed my Mother and me.

"Had we not better go and see who it is, ? (said she) the Servants are out." "I think we had." (replied I.) "Certainly, (added my Father) by all means." "Shall we go now?" (said my Mother.) "The sooner the better." (answered he). "Oh! let no time be lost." (cried I.)

A third more violent Rap than ever again assaulted our ears. "I am certain there is somebody knocking at the Door." (said my Mother.) "I think there must," (replied my Father) "I fancy the Servants are returned; (said I) I think I hear Mary going to the Door." "I'm glad of it (cried my Father) for I long to know who it is."

I was right in my Conjecture; for Mary instantly entering the Room, informed us that a young Gentleman & his Servant were at the Door, who had lossed their way, were very cold and begged leave to warm themselves by our fire.

"Wont you admit them?" (said I) "You have no objection, my Dear?" (said my Father.) "None in the World." (replied my Mother.)

Mary, without waiting for any further commands immediately left the room and quickly returned introducing the most beauteous and amiable Youth, I had ever beheld. The servant, She kept to herself.

My natural Sensibility had already been greatly affected by the sufferings of the unfortunate Stranger and no sooner did I first behold him, than I felt that on him the happiness or Misery of my future Life must depend.

adeiu.
LAURA.

Letter 6th
Laura to Marianne

The noble Youth informed us that his name was Lindsay—for particular reasons however I shall conceal it under that of Talbot. He told us that he was the son of an English Baronet, that his Mother had been many years no more and that he had a Sister of the middle size. "My Father (he continued) is a mean and mercenary wretch—it is only to such particular freinds as this Dear Party that I would thus betray his failings. Your Virtues my amiable Polydore (addressing himself to my father) yours Dear Claudia and yours my Charming Laura call on me to repose in you, my Confidence." We bowed. "My Father, seduced by the false glare of Fortune and the Deluding Pomp of Title, insisted on my giving my hand to Lady Dorothea. No never exclaimed I. Lady Dorothea is lovely and Engaging; I prefer no woman to her; but know Sir, that I scorn to marry her in compliance with your wishes. No! Never shall it be said that I obliged my Father,"

We all admired the noble Manliness of his reply. He continued.

"Sir Edward was surprized; he had perhaps little expected to meet with so spirited an opposition to his will. 'Where Edward in the name of wonder (said he) did you pick up this unmeaning Gibberish? You have been studying Novels I suspect.' I scorned to answer: it would have been beneath my Dignity. I mounted my Horse and followed by my faithful William set forwards for my Aunts."

"My Father's house is situated in Bedfordshire, my Aunt's in Middlesex, and tho' I flatter myself with being a tolerable proficienz in Geography, I know not how it happened, but I found myself entering this beautifull Vale which I find is in South Wales, when I had expected to have reached my Aunts."

"After having wandered some time on the Banks of the Uske without knowing which way to go, I began to lament my cruel Destiny in the bitterest and most pathetic Manner. It was now perfectly dark, not a single Star was there to direct my steps, and I know not what might have befallen me had I not at length discerned thro' the solemn Gloom that surrounded me a distant Light, which as I approached it, I discovered to be the chearfull Blaze of your fire. Impelled by the combination of Misfortunes under which I laboured, namely Fear, Cold and Hunger I hesitated not to ask admittance which at length I have gained; and now my Adorable Laura (continued he taking my Hand) when may I hope to receive that reward of all the painfull sufferings I have undergone during the course of my Attachment to you, to which I have ever aspired? Oh! when will you reward me with Yourself?"

"This instant, Dear and Amiable Edward." (replied I.). We were immediately united by my Father, who tho' he had never taken orders had been bred to the Church.

adeiu
LAURA.

Letter 7th
Laura to Marianne

We remained but a few Days after our Marriage, in the Vale of Uske. After taking an affecting Farewell of my father, my Mother and my Isabel, I accompanied Edward to his Aunt's in Middlesex. Philippa received us both with every expression of affectionate Love. My arrival was indeed a most agreable surprize to her as she had not only been totally ignorant of my Marriage with her Nephew, but had never even had the slightest idea of there being such a person in the World.

Augusta, the sister of Edward was on a visit to her when we arrived. I found her exactly what her Brother had described her to be—of the middle size. She received me with equal surprize though not with equal Cordiality, as Philippa. There was a Disagreable Coldness and Forbidding Reserve in her reception of me which was equally Distressing and Unexpected. None of that interesting Sensibility or amiable Simpathy in her Manners and Address to me which should have Distinguished our introduction to each other. Her Language was neither warm, nor affectionate, her expressions of regard were neither animated nor cordial; her arms were not opened to receive me to her Heart, tho' my own were extended to press her to mine.

A short Conversation between Augusta and her Brother, which I accidentally overheard encreased my Dislike to her, and convinced me that her Heart was no more formed for the soft ties of Love than for the endearing intercourse of Freindship.

"But do you think that my Father will ever be reconciled to this imprudent connection?" (said Augusta.)

"Augusta (replied the noble Youth) I thought you had a better opinion of me, than to imagine I would so abjectly degrade myself as to consider my Father's Concurrence in any of my Affairs, either of Consequence or concern to me. Tell me Augusta tell me with sincerity; did you ever know me consult his inclinations or follow his Advice in the least trifling Particular since the age of fifteen?"

"Edward (replied she) you are surely too diffident in your own praise. Since you were fifteen only!—My Dear Brother since you were five years old, I entirely acquit you of ever having willingly contributed to the Satisfaction of your Father. But still I am not without apprehensions of your being shortly obliged to degrade yourself in your own eyes by seeking a Support for your Wife in the Generosity of Sir Edward."

"Never, never Augusta will I so demean myself. (said Edward). Support! What Support will Laura want which she can receive from him?"

"Only those very insignificant ones of Victuals and Drink." (answered she.)

"Victuals and Drink! (replied my Husband in a most nobly contemtuous Manner) and dost thou then imagine that there is no other support for an exalted Mind (such as is my Laura's) than the mean and indelicate employment of Eating and Drinking?"

"None that I know of, so efficacious." (returned Augusta).

"And did you then never feel the pleasing Pangs of Love, Augusta? (replied my Edward). Does it appear impossible to your vile and corrupted Palate, to exist on Love? Can you not conceive the Luxury of living in every Distress that Poverty can inflict, with the object of your tenderest Affection?"

"You are too ridiculous (said Augusta) to argue with; perhaps however you may in time be convinced that. . . ."

Here I was prevented from hearing the remainder of her Speech, by the Appearance of a very Handsome Young Woman, who was ushered into the Room at the Door of which I had been listening. On hearing her announced by the Name of "Lady Dorothea", I instantly quitted my Post and followed her into the Parlour, for I well remembered that she was the Lady, proposed as a Wife for my Edward by the Cruel and Unrelenting Baronet.

Altho' Lady Dorothea's visit was nominally to Philippa and Augusta, yet I have some reason to imagine that (acquainted with the Marriage and arrival of Edward) to see me was a principal motive to it.

I soon perceived that tho' lovely and Elegant in her Person and tho' Easy and Polite in her Address, she was of that inferior order of Beings with regard to Delicate feeling, tender Sentiments, and refined Sensibility, of which Augusta was one.

She staid but half an hour and neither in the Course of her Visit, confided to me any of her Secret thoughts, nor requested me to confide in her, any of mine. You will easily imagine therefore my Dear Marianne that I could not feel any ardent Affection or very sincere Attachment for Lady Dorothea.

Adeiu
Laura

Letter 8th
Laura to Marianne, in continuation

Lady Dorothea had not left us long before another visitor as unexpected a one as her Ladyship, was announced. It was Sir Edward, who informed by Augusta of her Brother's marriage, came doubtless to reproach him for having dared to unite himself to me without his Knowledge. But Edward foreseeing his Design, approached him with heroic fortitude as soon as he entered the Room, and addressed him in the following Manner.

"Sir Edward, I know the motive of your Journey here—You come with the base Design of reproaching me for having entered into an indissoluble engagement with my Laura without your Consent—But Sir, I glory in the Act—. It is my greatest boast that I have incurred the Displeasure of my Father!"

So saying, he took my hand and whilst Sir Edward, Philippa, and Augusta were doubtless reflecting with Admiration on his undaunted Bravery, led me from the Parlour to his Father's Carriage, which yet remained at the Door and in which we were instantly conveyed from the pursuit of Sir Edward.

The Postilions had at first received orders only to take the London road; as soon as we had sufficiently reflected However, we ordered them to Drive to M————. the seat of Edward's most particular freind, which was but a few miles distant.

At M————. we arrived in a few hours; and on sending in our names were immediately admitted to Sophia, the Wife of Edward's freind. After having been deprived during the course of 3 weeks of a real freind (for such I term your Mother) imagine my transports at beholding one, most truly worthy of the Name. Sophia was rather above the middle size; most elegantly formed. A soft Languor spread over her lovely features, but increased their Beauty.—It was the Charectaristic of her Mind—. She was all Sensibility and Feeling. We flew into each others arms &

after having exchanged vows of mutual Friendship for the rest of our Lives, instantly unfolded to each other the most inward Secrets of our Hearts—. We were interrupted in this Delightfull Employment by the entrance of Augustus, (Edward's freind) who was just returned from a solitary ramble.

Never did I see such an affecting Scene as was the meeting of Edward & Augustus.

"My Life! my Soul!" (exclaimed the former) "My Adorable Angel!" (replied the latter) as they flew into each other's arms. It was too pathetic for the feelings of Sophia and myself—We fainted Alternately on a Sofa.

Adeiu

LAURA

Letter the 9th
From the Same to the Same

Towards the close of the Day we received the following Letter from Philippa.

"Sir Edward is greatly incensed by your abrupt departure; he has taken back Augusta with him to Bedfordshire. Much as I wish to enjoy again your charming society, I cannot determine to snatch you from that, of such dear & deserving Freinds—When your Visit to them is terminated, I trust you will return to the arms of your"

"PHILIPPA."

We returned a suitable answer to this affectionate Note & after thanking her for her kind invitation assured her that we would certainly avail ourselves of it, whenever we might have no other place to go to. Tho' certainly nothing could to any reasonable Being, have appeared more satisfactory, than so gratefull a reply to her invitation, yet I know not how it was, but she was certainly capricious enough to be displeased with our behaviour and in a few weeks after, either to revenge our Conduct, or releive her own solitude, married a young and illiterate Fortune-hunter. This imprudent Step (tho' we were sensible that it would probably deprive us of that fortune which Philippa had ever taught us to expect) could not on our own accounts, excite from our exalted Minds a single sigh; yet fearfull lest it might prove a source of endless misery to the deluded Bride, our trembling Sensibility was greatly affected when we were first informed of the Event. The affectionate Entreaties of Augustus and Sophia that we would for ever consider their House as our Home, easily prevailed on us to determine never more to leave them—. In the Society of my Edward & this Amiable Pair, I passed the happiest moments of my Life: Our time was most delightfully spent, in mutual Protestations of Freindship, and in vows of unalterable Love, in which we were secure from being interrupted, by intruding & disagreable Visitors, as Augustus & Sophia had on their first Entrance in the Neighbourhood, taken due care to inform the surrounding Families, that as their Happiness centered wholly in themselves, they wished for no other society. But alas! my Dear Marianne such Happiness as I then enjoyed was too perfect to be lasting. A most severe & unexpected Blow at once destroyed every Sensation of Pleasure. Convinced as you must be from what I have already told you concerning Augustus & Sophia, that there never were a happier Couple, I need not I imagine inform you that their union had been contrary to the inclinations of their Cruel & Mercenary Parents; who had vainly endeavoured with obstinate Perseverance to force them into a Marriage with those whom they had ever abhorred, but with an Heroic Fortitude worthy to be related & Admired, they had both, constantly refused to submit to such despotic Power.

After having so nobly disentangled themselves from the Shackles of Parental Authority, by a Clandestine Marriage, they were determined never to forfeit the good opinion they had gained in the World, in so doing, by accepting any proposals of reconciliation that might be offered them by their Fathers—to this farther tryal of their noble independance however they never were exposed.

They had been married but a few months when our visit to them commenced during which time they had been amply supported by a considerable sum of Money which Augustus had gracefully purloined from his Unworthy father's Escritoire, a few days before his union with Sophia.

By our arrival their Expences were considerably encreased tho' their means for supplying them were then nearly exhausted. But they, Exalted Creatures! scorned to reflect a moment on their pecuniary Distresses & would have blushed at the idea of paying their Debts.—Alas! what was their Reward for such disinterested Behaviour. The beautifull Augustus was arrested and we were all undone. Such perfidious Treachery in the merciless perpetrators of the Deed will shock your gentle nature Dearest Marianne as much as it then affected the Delicate Sensibility of Edward, Sophia, your Laura, & of Augustus himself. To compleat such unparalelled Barbarity we were informed that an Execution in the House would shortly take place. Ah! what could we do but what we did! We sighed & fainted on the Sofa.

Adeiu
LAURA

Letter 10th
Laura in continuation

When we were somewhat recovered from the overpowering Effusions of our Grief, Edward desired that we would consider what was the most prudent step to be taken in our unhappy situation while he repaired to his imprisoned freind to lament over his misfortunes. We promised that we would, & he set forwards on his Journey to Town. During his Absence we faithfully complied with his Desire & after the most mature Deliberation, at length agreed that the best thing we could do was to leave the House; of which we every moment expected the Officers of Justice to take possession. We waited therefore with the greatest impatience, for the return of Edward in order to impart to him the result of our Deliberations—. But no Edward appeared—. In vain did we count the tedious Moments of his Absence—in vain did we weep—in vain even did we sigh—no Edward returned—. This was too cruel, too unexpected a Blow to our Gentle Sensibility—. we could not support it—we could only faint—. At length collecting all the Resolution I was Mistress of, I arose & after packing up some necessary Apparel for Sophia & myself, I dragged her to a Carriage I had ordered & instantly we set out for London. As the Habitation of Augustus was within twelve miles of Town, it was not long e'er we arrived there, & no sooner had we entered Holbourn than letting down one of the Front Glasses I enquired of every decent-looking Person that we passed "If they had seen my Edward"?

But as we drove too rapidly to allow them to answer my repeated Enquiries, I gained little, or indeed, no information concerning him. "Where am I to Drive?" said the Postilion. "To Newgate Gentle Youth (replied I), to see Augustus." "Oh! no, no, (exclaimed Sophia) I cannot go to Newgate; I shall not be able to support the sight of my Augustus in so cruel a confinement—my feelings are sufficiently shocked by the *recital*, of his Distress, but to behold it will overpower my Sensibility." As I perfectly agreed with her in the Justice of her Sentiments the Postilion was instantly directed to return into the Country. You may perhaps have been somewhat surprised my Dearest Marianne, that in the Distress I then endured, destitute of any Support, & unprovided with any Habitation, I should never once have remembered my Father & Mother or my paternal Cottage in the Vale of Uske. To account for this seeming forgetfullness I must inform you of a trifling Circumstance concerning them which I have as yet never mentioned—. The death of my Parents a few weeks after my Departure, is the circumstance I allude to. By their decease I became the lawfull Inheritress of their House & Fortune. But alas! the House had never been their own & their Fortune had only been an Annuity on their own Lives. Such is the Depravity of the World! To your Mother I should have returned with Pleasure, should have been happy to have introduced to her, my Charming Sophia & should have with Chearfullness have passed the remainder of my Life in their dear Society in the Vale of Uske, had not one obstacle to the execution of so agreable a Scheme, intervened; which was the Marriage & Removal of your Mother to a Distant part of Ireland.

Adeiu.
LAURA.

Letter 11th
Laura in continuation

"I have a Relation in Scotland (said Sophia to me as we left London) who I am certain would not hesitate in receiving me." "Shall I order the Boy to drive there?" said I—but instantly recollecting myself, exclaimed "Alas I fear it will be too long a Journey for the Horses." Unwilling however to act only from my own inadequate Knowledge of the Strength & Abilities of Horses, I consulted the Postilion, who was entirely of my Opinion concerning the Affair. We therefore determined to change Horses at the next Town & to travel Post the remainder of the Journey.—. When we arrived at the last Inn we were to stop at, which was but a few miles from the House of Sophia's Relation, unwilling to intrude our Society on him unexpected & unthought of, we wrote a very elegant & well-penned Note to him containing an Account of our Destitute & melancholy Situation, and of our intention to spend some months with him in Scotland. As soon as we had dispatched this letter, we immediately prepared to follow it in person & were stepping into the Carriage for that Purpose when our Attention was attracted by the Entrance of a coroneted Coach & 4 into the Inn-yard. A Gentleman considerably advanced in years, descended from it—. At his first Appearance my Sensibility was wonderfully affected & e'er I had gazed at him a 2d time, an instinctive Sympathy whispered to my Heart, that he was my Grandfather.

Convinced that I could not be mistaken in my conjecture I instantly sprang from the Carriage I had just entered, & following the Venerable Stranger into the Room he had been shewn to, I threw myself on my knees before him & besought him to acknowledge me as his Grand Child.—He started, & after having attentively examined my features, raised me from the Ground & throwing his Grand-fatherly arms around my neck, exclaimed, "Acknowledge thee! Yes dear resemblance of my Laurina & my Laurina's Daughter, sweet image of my Claudia & my Claudia's Mother, I do acknowledge thee as the Daughter of the one & the Grandaughter of the other." While he was thus tenderly embracing me, Sophia astonished at my precipitate Departure, entered the Room in search of me—. No sooner had she caught the eye of the venerable Peer, than he exclaimed with every mark of Astonishment—"Another Grandaughter! Yes, yes, I see you are the Daughter of my Laurina's eldest Girl; Your resemblance to the beauteous Matilda sufficiently proclaims it." "Oh.!" replied Sophia, "when I first beheld you the instinct of Nature whispered me that we were in some degree related—But whether Grandfathers, or Grandmothers, I could not pretend to determine." He folded her in his arms, and whilst they were tenderly embracing, the Door of the Apartment opened and a most beautifull Young Man appeared. On perceiving him Lord St. Clair started and retreating back a few paces, with uplifted Hands, said, "Another Grandchild! What an unexpected Happiness is this! to discover in the space of 3 minutes, as many of my Descendants! This, I am certain is Philander the son of my Laurina's 3d Girl the amiable Bertha; there wants now but the presence of Gustavus to compleat the Union of my Laurina's Grand-Children".

"And here he is; (said a Gracefull Youth who that instant entered the room) here is the Gustavus you desire to see. I am the son of Agatha your Laurina's 4th & Youngest Daughter." "I see you are indeed; replied Lord St. Clair—But tell me (continued he looking fearfully towards the Door) tell me, have I any other Grand-Children in the House." "None my Lord." "Then I will provide for you all without further delay—Here are 4 Banknotes of 50£ each—Take them & remember I have done the Duty of a Grandfather—." He instantly left the Room & immediately afterwards the House.

Adeiu.

Laura.

Letter the
12th Laura in continuation

You may imagine how greatly we were surprised by the sudden departure of Lord St. Clair. "Ignoble Grand-sire!" exclaimed Sophia. "Unworthy Grandfather!" said I, & instantly fainted in each other's arms. How long we remained in this situation I know not; but when we recovered we found ourselves alone, without either Gustavus, Philander or the Bank-notes. As we were deploring our unhappy fate, the Door of the Apartment opened & "Macdonald" was announced. He was Sophia's cousin. The haste with which he came to our releif so soon after the receipt of our Note, spoke so greatly in his favour that I hesitated not to pronounce him at first sight, a tender & Simpathetic Freind. Alas! he little deserved the name—for though he told us that he was much concerned at our Misfortunes, yet by his own account it appeared that the perusal of them, had neither drawn from him a single sigh, nor induced him to bestow one curse on our vindictive Stars.—. He told Sophia that his Daughter depended on her returning with him to Macdonald-Hall, & that as his Cousin's freind he should be happy to see me there also. To Macdonald-Hall, therefore, we went, and were received with great kindness by Janetta the daughter of Macdonald, & the Mistress of the Mansion. Janetta was then only fifteen; naturally well disposed, endowed with a susceptible Heart, and a simpathetic Disposition, she might, had these amiable Qualities been properly encouraged, have been an ornament to human Nature; but unfortunately her Father possessed not a soul sufficiently exalted to admire so promising a Disposition, and had endeavoured by every means in his power to prevent its encreasing with her Years. He had actually so far extinguished the natural noble Sensibility of her Heart, as to prevail on her to accept an offer from a young man of his Recommendation. They were to be married in a few months, and Graham, was in the House when we arrived. *We* soon saw through his Character.—. He was just such a Man as one might have expected to be the choice of Macdonald. They said he was Sensible, well-informed, and Agreable; we did not pretend to Judge of such trifles, but as we were convinced he had no soul, that he had never read the Sorrows of Werter, & that his Hair bore not the slightest resemblance to Auburn, we were certain that Janetta could feel no affection for him, or at least that she ought to feel none. The very circumstance of his being her father's choice too, was so much in his disfavour, that had he been deserving her, in every other respect yet *that* of itself ought to have been a sufficient reason in the Eyes of Janetta for rejecting him. These considerations we were determined to represent to her in their proper light & doubted not of meeting with the desired success from one naturally so well disposed, whose errors in the Affair had only arisen from a want of proper confidence in her own opinion, & a suitable contempt of her father's. We found her indeed all that our warmest wishes could have hoped for; we had no difficulty to convince her that it was impossible she could love Graham, or that it was her duty to disobey her Father; the only thing at which she rather seemed to hesitate was our assertion that she must be attached to some other Person. For some time, she persevered in declaring that she knew no other young Man for whom she had the smallest Affection; but upon explaining the impossibility of such a thing she said that she beleived she *did like* Captain M'Kenzie better than any one she knew besides. This confession satisfied us and after having enumerated the good Qualities of M'Kenzie & assured her that she was violently in love with him, we desired to know whether he had ever in any wise declared his Affection to her.

"So far from having ever declared it, I have no reason to imagine that he has ever felt any for me." said Janetta. "That he certainly adores you (replied Sophia) there can be no doubt—. The Attachment must be reciprocal—. Did he never gaze on you with Admiration—tenderly press your hand—drop an involuntary tear—& leave the room abruptly?" "Never (replied She) that I remember—he has always left the room indeed when his visit has been ended, but has never gone away particularly abruptly or without making a bow". "Indeed my Love (said I) you must be mistaken—: for it is absolutely impossible that he should ever have left you but with Confusion, Despair, & Precipitation—. Consider but for a moment Janetta, & you must be convinced how absurd it is to suppose that he could ever make a Bow, or behave like any other Person." Having settled this Point to our satisfaction, the next we took into consideration was, to determine in what manner we should inform M'Kenzie of the favourable Opinion Janetta entertained of him.—. We at length agreed to acquaint him with it by an anonymous Letter which Sophia drew up in the following Manner.

"Oh! happy Lover of the beautifull Janetta, oh! enviable Possessor of *her* Heart whose hand is destined to another, why do you thus delay a confession of your Attachment to the amiable Object of it? Oh! consider that a few weeks will at once put an end to every flattering Hope that you may now entertain, by uniting the unfortunate Victim of her father's Cruelty to the execrable & detested Graham."

"Alas! why do you thus so cruelly connive at the projected Misery of her & of yourself by delaying to communicate that scheme which had doubtless long possessed your imagination? A secret Union will at once secure the felicity of both."

The amiable M'Kenzie, whose modesty as he afterwards assured us had been the only reason of his having so long concealed the violence of his affection for Janetta, on receiving this Billet flew on the wings of Love to Macdonald-Hall, and so powerfully pleaded his Attachment to her who inspired it, that after a few more private interviews, Sophia & I experienced the Satisfaction of seeing them depart for Gretna-Green, which they chose for the celebration of their Nuptials, in preference to any other place although it was at a considerable distance from Macdonald-Hall.

Adeiu—

LAURA—

Letter the 13th
Laura in Continuation

THEY had been gone nearly a couple of Hours, before either Macdonald or Graham had entertained any suspicion of the affair—. And they might not even then have suspected it, but for the following little Accident. Sophia happening one Day to open a private Drawer in Macdonald's Library with one of her own keys, discovered that it was the Place where he kept his Papers of consequence & amongst them some bank notes of considerable amount. This discovery she imparted to me; and having agreed together that it would be a proper treatment of so vile a Wretch as Macdonald to deprive him of money, perhaps dishonestly gained, it was determined that the next time we should either of us happen to go that way, we would take one or more of the Bank notes from the drawer. This well-meant Plan we had often successfully put in Execution; but alas! on the very day of Janetta's Escape, as Sophia was majestically removing the 5th Bank-note from the Drawer to her own purse, she was suddenly most impertinently interrupted in her employment by the entrance of Macdonald himself, in a most abrupt & precipitate Manner. Sophia (who though naturally all winning sweetness could when occasions demanded it call forth the Dignity of her Sex) instantly put on a most forbidding look, & darting an angry frown on the undaunted Culprit, demanded in a haughty tone of voice "Wherefore her retirement was thus insolently broken in on?" The unblushing Macdonald, without even endeavouring to exculpate himself from the crime he was charged with, meanly endeavoured to reproach Sophia with ignobly defrauding him of his Money. The dignity of Sophia was wounded; "Wretch (exclaimed she, hastily replacing the Bank-note in the Drawer) how darest thou to accuse me of an Act, of which the bare idea makes me blush?" The base wretch was still unconvinced & continued to upbraid the justly-offended Sophia in such opprobrious Language, that at length he so greatly provoked the gentle sweetness of her Nature, as to induce her to revenge herself on him by informing him of Janetta's Elopement, and of the active Part we had both taken in the Affair. At this period of their Quarrel I entered the Library and was as you may imagine equally offended as Sophia at the ill-grounded Accusations of the malevolent and contemptible Macdonald. "Base Miscreant (cried I) how canst thou thus undauntedly endeavour to sully the spotless reputation of such bright Excellence? Why dost thou not suspect *my* innocence as soon?" "Be satisfied Madam (replied he) I *do* suspect it, & therefore must desire that you will both leave this House in less than half an hour."

"We shall go willingly; (answered Sophia) our hearts have long detested thee, & nothing but our freindship for thy Daughter could have induced us to remain so long beneath thy roof."

"Your Freindship for my Daughter has indeed been most powerfully exerted by throwing her into the arms of an unprincipled Fortune-hunter." (replied he)

"Yes, (exclaimed I) amidst every misfortune, it will afford us some consolation to reflect that by this one act of Freindship to Janetta, we have amply discharged every obligation that we have received from her father."

"It must indeed be a most gratefull reflection, to your exalted minds." (said he.)

As soon as we had packed up our wardrobe & valuables, we left Macdonald Hall, & after having walked about a mile & a half we sate down by the side of a clear limpid stream to refresh our exhausted limbs. The place was suited to meditation.—. A Grove of full-grown Elms sheltered us from the East—. A Bed of full-grown Nettles from the West—. Before us ran the murmuring brook & behind us ran the turn-pike road. We were in a mood for contemplation & in a Disposition to enjoy so beautifull a spot. A mutual Silence which had for some time reigned between us, was at length broke by my exclaiming—"What a lovely Scene! Alas why are not Edward & Augustus here to enjoy its Beauties with us?".

"Ah! my beloved Laura (cried Sophia) for pity's sake forbear recalling to my remembrance the unhappy situation of my imprisoned Husband. Alas, what would I not give to learn the fate of my Augustus! to know if he is still in Newgate, or if he is yet hung. But never shall I be able so far to conquer my tender sensibility as to enquire after him. Oh! do not I beseech you ever let me again hear you repeat his beloved name—. It affects me too deeply—. I cannot bear to hear him mentioned, it wounds my feelings."

"Excuse me my Sophia for having thus unwillingly offended you—" replied I—and then changing the conversation, desired her to admire the Noble Grandeur of the Elms which Sheltered us from the Eastern Zephyr. "Alas! my Laura (returned she) avoid so melancholy a subject, I intreat you.— Do not again wound my Sensibility by Observations on those elms. They remind me of Augustus—. He was like them, tall, magestic—he possessed that noble grandeur which you admire in them."

I was silent, fearfull lest I might any more unwillingly distress her by fixing on any other subject of conversation which might again remind her of Augustus.

"Why do you not speak my Laura?" (said she after a short pause) "I cannot support this silence—you must not leave me to my own reflections; they ever recur to Augustus."

"What a beautifull Sky! (said I) How charmingly is the azure varied by those delicate streaks of white!"

"Oh! my Laura (replied she hastily withdrawing her Eyes from a momentary glance at the sky) do not thus distress me by calling my Attention to an object which so cruelly reminds me of my Augustus's blue sattin Waist-coat striped with white! In pity to your unhappy freind avoid a subject so distressing." What could I do? The feelings of Sophia were at that time so exquisite, & the tenderness she felt for Augustus so poignant that I had not the power to start any other topic, justly fearing that it might in some unforseen manner again awaken all her sensibility by directing her thoughts to her Husband.—Yet to be silent would be cruel; She had intreated me to talk.

From this Dilemma I was most fortunately releived by an accident truly apropos; it was the lucky overturning of a Gentleman's Phaeton, on the road which ran murmuring behind us. It was a most fortunate Accident as it diverted the Attention of Sophia from the melancholy reflections which she had been before indulging. We instantly quitted our seats & ran to the rescue of those who but a few moments before had been in so elevated a situation as a fashionably high Phaeton, but who were now laid low and sprawling in the Dust—. "What an ample subject for reflection on the uncertain Enjoyments of this World, would not that Phaeton & the Life of Cardinal Wolsey afford a thinking Mind!" said I to Sophia as we were hastening to the field of Action.

She had not time to answer me for every thought was now engaged by the horrid Spectacle before us. Two Gentlemen most elegantly attired but weltering in their blood was what first struck our Eyes—we approached—they were Edward & Augustus—Yes dearest Marianne they were our Husbands. Sophia shreiked & fainted on the Ground—I screamed and instantly ran mad—. We remained thus mutually deprived of our Senses some minutes, & on regaining them were deprived of them again—. For an Hour & a Quarter did we continue in this unfortunate Situation—Sophia fainting every moment & I running Mad as often. At length a

Groan from the hapless Edward (who alone retained any share of Life) restored us to ourselves—. Had we indeed before imagined that either of them lived, we should have been more sparing of our Greif—but as we had supposed when we first beheld them that they were no more, we knew that nothing could remain to be done but what we were about—. No sooner therefore did we hear my Edward's groan than postponing our Lamentations for the present, we hastily ran to the Dear Youth and kneeling on each side of him implored him not to die—. "Laura (said He fixing his now languid Eyes on me) I fear I have been overturned."

I was overjoyed to find him yet sensible—.

"Oh! tell me Edward (said I) tell me I beseech you before you die, what has befallen you since that unhappy Day in which Augustus was arrested & we were separated—"

"I will" (said he) and instantly fetching a Deep sigh, expired—. Sophia immediately sunk again into a swoon—. *My* Greif was more audible, My voice faltered, My Eyes assumed a vacant Stare, My face became as pale as Death, and my Senses were considerably impaired—.

"Talk not to me of Phaetons (said I, raving in a frantic, incoherent manner)— Give me a violin—. I'll play to him & sooth him in his melancholy Hours— Beware ye gentle Nymphs of Cupid's Thunderbolts, avoid the piercing Shafts of Jupiter—Look at that Grove of Firs—I see a Leg of Mutton—They told me Edward was not Dead; but they deceived me—they took him for a Cucumber—" Thus I continued wildly exclaiming on my Edward's death—. For two Hours did I rave thus madly and should not then have left off, as I was not in the least fatigued, had not Sophia who was just recovered from her swoon, intreated me to consider that Night was now approaching and that the Damps began to fall. "And whither shall we go (said I) to shelter us from either"? "To that white Cottage." (replied she pointing to a neat building which rose up amidst the Grove of Elms & which I had not before observed—) I agreed & we instantly walked to it—we knocked at the door—it was opened by an old Woman; on being requested to afford us a Night's Lodging, she informed us that her House was but small, that she had only two Bed-rooms, but that However we should be wellcome to one of them. We were satisfied & followed the good Woman into the House where we were greatly cheered by the sight of a comfortable fire—. She was a Widow & had only one Daughter, who was then just Seventeen—One of the best of ages; but alas! she was very plain & her name was Bridget. . . . . . . Nothing therefore could be expected from her—she could not be supposed to possess either exalted Ideas, Delicate Feelings or refined Sensibilities—She was nothing more than a mere good-tempered, civil & obliging Young Woman; as such we could scarcely dislike her—she was only an Object of Contempt—.

Adeiu
LAURA—

Letter the 14th
Laura in continuation

ARM yourself my amiable Young Freind with all the philosophy you are Mistress of; summon up all the fortitude you possess, for Alas! in the perusal of the following Pages your sensibility will be most severely tried. Ah! what were the Misfortunes I had before experienced & which I have already related to you, to the one I am now going to inform you of. The Death of my Father, my Mother, and my Husband though almost more than my gentle Nature could support, were trifles in comparison to the misfortune I am now proceeding to relate. The morning after our arrival at the Cottage, Sophia complained of a violent pain in her delicate limbs, accompanied with a disagreable Head-ake. She attributed it to a cold caught by her continued faintings in the open Air as the Dew was falling the Evening before. This I feared was but too probably the case; since how could it be otherwise accounted for that I should have escaped the same indisposition, but by supposing that the bodily Exertions I had undergone in my repeated fits of frenzy, had so effectually circulated & warmed my Blood as to make me proof against the chilling Damps of Night, whereas, Sophia lying totally inactive on the Ground must have been exposed to all their Severity. I was most seriously alarmed by her illness which trifling as it may appear to you, a certain instinctive Sensibility whispered me, would in the End be fatal to her.

Alas! my fears were but too fully justified; she grew gradually worse & I daily became more alarmed for her.—At length she was obliged to confine herself solely to the Bed allotted us by our worthy Landlady—. Her disorder turned to a galloping Consumption & in a few Days carried her off. Amidst all my Lamentations for her (& violent you may suppose they were) I yet received some consolation in the reflection of my having paid every Attention to her, that could be offered, in her illness. I had wept over her every Day—had bathed her sweet face with my tears & had pressed her fair Hands continually in mine—. "My beloved Laura (said she to me a few Hours before she died) take warning from my unhappy End & avoid the imprudent conduct which has occasioned it . . beware of fainting-fits . . Though at the time they may be refreshing & Agreable yet beleive me they will in the end, if too often repeated & at improper seasons, prove destructive to your Constitution . . . . . My fate will teach you this . . I die a Martyr to my greif for the loss of Augustus. . . . One fatal swoon has cost me my Life. . . . Beware of swoons Dear Laura . . . A frenzy fit is not one quarter so pernicious; it is an exercise to the Body & if not too violent, is I dare say conducive to Health in its consequences—Run mad as often as you chuse; but do not faint—".

These were the last words she ever adressed to me . . . It was her dieing Advice to her afflicted Laura, who has ever most faithfully adhered to it.

After having attended my lamented freind to her Early Grave, I immediately (tho' late at night) left the detested Village in which she died, & near which had expired my Husband & Augustus. I had not walked many yards from it before I was overtaken by a Stage-Coach, in which I instantly took a place, determined to proceed in it to Edinburgh, where I hoped to find some kind pitying Freind who would receive and comfort me in my Afflictions.

It was so dark when I entered the Coach that I could not distinguish the Number of my Fellow-travellers; I could only perceive that they were Many. Regardless however of any thing concerning them, I gave myself up to my own sad Reflections. A general Silence prevailed—A Silence, which was by nothing interrupted but by the loud & repeated snores of one of the Party.

"What an illiterate villain must that Man be! (thought I to myself) What a total Want of delicate refinement must he have who can thus shock our senses by such a brutal Noise! He must I am certain be capable of every bad Action! There is no crime too black for such a Character!" Thus reasoned I within myself, & doubtless such were the reflections of my fellow travellers.

At length, returning Day enabled me to behold the unprincipled Scoundrel who had so violently disturbed my feelings. It was Sir Edward the father of my Deceased Husband. By his side, sate Augusta, & on the same seat with me were your Mother & Lady Dorothea. Imagine my Surprise at finding myself thus seated amongst my old Acquaintance. Great as was my astonishment, it was yet increased, when on look out of Windows, I beheld the Husband of Philippa, with Philippa by his side, on the Coach-box, & when on looking behind, I beheld, Philander & Gustavus in the Basket. "Oh! Heavens, (exclaimed I) is it possible that I should so unexpectedly be surrounded by my nearest Relations and Connections"? These words roused the rest of the Party, and every eye was directed to the corner in which I sat. "Oh! my Isabel (continued I throwing myself across Lady Dorothea into her arms) receive once more to your Bosom the unfortunate Laura. Alas! when we last parted in the Vale of Usk, I was happy in being united to the best of Edwards; I had then a Father and a Mother, & had never known misfortunes—But now deprived of every freind but you—".

"What! (interrupted Augusta) is my Brother dead then? Tell us I intreat you what is become of him?" "Yes, cold & insensible Nymph, (replied I) that luckless Swain your Brother, is no more, & you may now glory in being the Heiress of Sir Edward's fortune."

Although I had always despised her from the Day I had overheard her conversation with my Edward, yet in civility I complied with hers & Sir Edward's intreaties that I would inform them of the whole melancholy Affair. They were greatly shocked—Even the obdurate Heart of Sir Edward & the insensible one of Augusta, were touched with Sorrow, by the unhappy tale. At the request of your Mother I related to them every other misfortune which had befallen me since we parted.

Of the imprisonment of Augustus & the absence of Edward—of our arrival in Scotland—of our unexpected Meeting with our Grandfather and our cousins—of our visit to Macdonald-Hall—of the singular Service we there performed towards Janetta—of her Fathers ingratitude for it . . . . . of his inhuman Behaviour, unaccountable suspicions, & barbarous treatment of us, in obliging us to leave the House . . . . . of our Lamentations on the loss of Edward & Augustus & finally of the melancholy Death of my beloved Companion.

Pity & Surprise were strongly depictured in your Mother's Countenance, during the whole of my narration, but I am sorry to say, that to the eternal reproach of her Sensibility, the latter infinitely predominated. Nay, faultless as my Conduct had certainly been during the whole Course of my late Misfortunes & Adventures, she pretended to find fault with my Behaviour in many of the situations in which I had been placed. As I was sensible myself, that I had always behaved in a manner which reflected Honour on my Feelings & Refinement, I paid little attention to what she said, & desired her to satisfy my Curiosity by informing me how she came there, instead of wounding my spotless reputation with unjustifiable Reproaches. As soon as she had complied with my wishes in this particular & had given me an accurate detail of every thing that had befallen her since our separation (the particulars of which if you are not already acquainted with, your Mother will give you) I applied to Augusta for the same information respecting herself, Sir Edward & Lady Dorothea.

She told me that having a considerable taste for the Beauties of Nature, her curiosity to behold the delightful scenes it exhibited in that part of the World had been so much raised by Gilpin's Tour to the Highlands, that she had prevailed on her Father to undertake a Tour of Scotland & had persuaded Lady Dorothea to accompany them. That they had arrived at Edinburgh a few days before & from thence had made daily Excursions into the Country around in the Stage Coach they were then in, from one of which Excursions they were at that time returning. My next enquiries were concerning Philippa & her Husband, the latter of whom I learned having spent all her fortune, had recourse for subsistance to the talent in which, he had always most excelled, namely, Driving, & that having sold every thing which belonged to them except their Coach, had converted it into a Stage, & in order to be removed from any of his former Acquaintance, had driven it to Edinburgh from whence he went to Sterling every other Day; That Philippa still retaining her affection for her ungratefull Husband, had followed him to Scotland & generally accompanied him in his little Excursions to Sterling. "It has only been to throw a little money into their Pockets (continued Augusta) that my Father has always travelled in their Coach to veiw the beauties of the Country since our arrival in Scotland—for it would certainly have been much more agreable to us, to visit the Highlands in a Postchaise than merely to travel from Edinburgh to Sterling & from Sterling to Edinburgh every other Day in a crouded & uncomfortable Stage." I perfectly agreed with her in her sentiments on the Affair, & secretly blamed Sir Edward for thus sacrificing his Daughter's pleasure for the sake of a ridiculous old Woman whose folly in marrying so young a Man ought to be punished. His Behaviour however was entirely of a peice with his general Character; for what could be expected from a Man who possessed not the smallest atom of Sensibility, who scarcely knew the meaning of Simpathy, & who actually snored—.

Adeiu
LAURA.

Letter the 15th
Laura in continuation

When we arrived at the town where we were to Breakfast, I was determined to speak with Philander & Gustavus, & to that purpose as soon as I left the Carriage, I went to the Basket & tenderly enquired after their Health, expressing my fears of the uneasiness of their Situation. At first they seemed rather confused at my Appearance dreading no doubt that I might call them to account for the money which our Grandfather had left me & which they had unjustly deprived me of, but finding that I mentioned nothing of the Matter, they desired me to step into the Basket as we might there converse with greater ease. Accordingly I entered & whilst the rest of the party were devouring Green tea & buttered toast, we feasted ourselfs in a more refined & Sentimental Manner by a confidential Conversation. I informed them of every thing which had befallen me during the course of my Life, and at my request they related to me every incident of theirs.

"We are the sons as you already know, of the two youngest Daughters which Lord St. Clair had by Laurina an italian opera girl. Our mothers could neither of them exactly ascertain who were our fathers; though it is generally beleived that Philander, is the son of one Philip Jones a Bricklayer and that my father was Gregory Staves a Staymaker of Edinburgh. This is however of little consequence, for as our Mothers were certainly never married to either of them, it reflects no Dishonour on our Blood which is of a most ancient & unpolluted kind. Bertha (the Mother of Philander) & Agatha (my own Mother) always lived together. They were neither of them very rich; their united fortunes had originally amounted to nine thousand Pounds, but as they had always lived upon the principal of it, when we were fifteen it was diminished to nine Hundred. This nine Hundred, they always kept in a Drawer in one of the Tables which stood in our common sitting Parlour, for the Convenience of having it always at Hand. Whether it was from this circumstance, of its being easily taken, or from a wish of being independant, or from an excess of Sensibility (for which we were always remarkable) I cannot now determine, but certain it is that when we had reached our 15th year, we took the Nine Hundred Pounds & ran away. Having obtained this prize we were determined to manage it with eoconomy & not to spend it either with folly or Extravagance. To this purpose we therefore divided it into nine parcels, one of which we devoted to Victuals, the 2d to Drink, the 3d to Housekeeping, the 4th to Carriages, the 5th to Horses, the 6th to Servants, the 7th to Amusements, the 8th to Cloathes & the 9th to Silver Buckles. Having thus arranged our Expences for two Months (for we expected to make the nine Hundred Pounds last as long) we hastened to London & had the good luck to spend it in 7 weeks & a Day which was 6 Days sooner than we had intended. As soon as we had thus happily disencumbered ourselves from the weight of so much Money, we began to think of returning to our Mothers, but accidentally hearing that they were both starved to death, we gave over the design & determined to engage ourselves to some strolling Company of Players, as we had always a turn for the Stage. Accordingly we offered our services to one & were accepted; our Company was indeed rather small, as it consisted only of the Manager his wife & ourselves, but there were fewer to pay and the only inconvenience attending it was the Scarcity of Plays which for want of People to fill the Characters, we could perform.—. We did not mind trifles however—. One of our most admired Performances was *Macbeth,* in which we were truly great. The Manager always played *Banquo* himself, his Wife my *Lady Macbeth.* I did the *Three Witches* & Philander acted *all the rest.* To say the truth this tragedy was not only the Best, but the only Play we ever performed; & after having acted it all over England, and Wales, we came to Scotland to exhibit it over the remainder of Great Britain. We happened to be quartered in that very Town, where you came and met your Grandfather—. We were in the Inn-yard when his Carriage entered & perceiving by the Arms to whom it belonged, & knowing that Lord St. Clair was our Grandfather, we agreed to endeavour to get something from him by discovering the Relationship—. You know how well it succeeded—. Having obtained the two Hundred Pounds, we instantly left the Town, leaving our Manager & his wife to act *Macbeth* by themselves, & took the road to Sterling, where we spent our little fortune with great *eclat.* We are now returning to Edinburgh to get some preferment in the Acting way; & such my Dear Cousin is our History."

I thanked the amiable Youth for his entertaining Narration, & after expressing my Wishes for their Welfare & Happiness, left them in their little Habitation & returned to my other Freinds who impatiently expected me.

My Adventures are now drawing to a close my dearest Marianne; at least for the present.

When we arrived at Edinburgh Sir Edward told me that as the Widow of his Son, he desired I would accept from his Hands of four Hundred a year. I graciously promised that I would, but could not help observing that the unsimpathetic Baronet offered it more on account of my being the Widow of Edward than in being the refined & Amiable Laura.

I took up my Residence in a romantic Village in the Highlands of Scotland, where I have ever since continued, & where I can uninterrupted by unmeaning Visits, indulge in a melancholy solitude, my unceasing Lamentations for the Death of my Father, my Mother, my Husband & my Freind.

Augusta has been for several Years united to Graham the Man of all others most suited to her; she became acquainted with him during her stay in Scotland.

Sir Edward in hopes of gaining an Heir to his Title & Estate, at the same time married Lady Dorothea—. His wishes have been answered.

Philander & Gustavus, after having raised their reputation by their Performances in the Theatrical Line at Edinburgh, removed to Covent Garden, where they still Exhibit under the assumed names of *Lewis & Quick.*

Philippa has long paid the Debt of Nature, Her Husband however still continues to drive the Stage-Coach from Edinburgh to Sterling:—

Adeiu my Dearest Marianne.
LAURA—

FINIS

June 13th 1790

Lesley Castle

an unfinished Novel in Letters

To Henry Thomas Austen Esqre.

SIR

I am now availing myself of the Liberty you have frequently honoured me with of dedicating one of my Novels to you. That it is unfinished, I greive; yet fear that from me, it will always remain so; that as far as it is carried, it Should be so trifling and so unworthy of you, is another concern to your obliged humble

Servant
THE AUTHOR

Messrs Demand & Co—please to pay Jane Austen Spinster the sum of one hundred guineas on account of your Humbl. Servant.

H T AUSTEN.

£105. 0. 0

Letter The first is from
Miss Margaret Lesley to Miss Charlotte Lutterell.

Lesley-Castle Janry 3d—1792.

MY Brother has just left us. "Matilda (said he at parting) you and Margaret will I am certain take all the care of my dear little one, that she might have received from an indulgent, an affectionate an amiable Mother." Tears rolled down his cheeks as he spoke these words—the remembrance of her, who had so wantonly disgraced the Maternal character and so openly violated the conjugal Duties, prevented his adding anything farther; he embraced his sweet Child and after saluting Matilda & Me hastily broke from us and seating himself in his Chaise, pursued the road to Aberdeen. Never was there a better young Man! Ah! how little did he deserve the misfortunes he has experienced in the Marriage state. So good a Husband to so bad a Wife! for you know my dear Charlotte that the Worthless Louisa left him, her Child & reputation a few weeks ago in company with Danvers &[1] dishonour. Never was there a sweeter face, a finer form, or a less amiable Heart than Louisa owned! Her child already possesses the personal charms of her unhappy Mother! May she inherit from her Father all his mental ones! Lesley is at present but five and twenty, and has already given himself up to melancholy and Despair; what a difference between him and his Father! Sir George is 57 and still remains the Beau, the flighty stripling, the gay Lad and sprightly Youngster, that his Son was really about five years back, and that *he* has affected to appear ever since my remembrance. While our father is fluttering about the streets of London, gay, dissipated, and Thoughtless at the age of 57, Matilda and I continue secluded from Mankind in our old and Mouldering Castle, which is situated two miles from Perth on a bold projecting Rock, and commands an extensive view of the Town and its delightful Environs. But tho' retired from almost all the World, (for we visit no one but the M'Leods, the M'Kenzies, the M'Phersons, the M'Cartneys, the M'donalds, The M'Kinnons, the M'lellans, the M'Kays, the Macbeths and the Macduffs) we are neither dull nor unhappy; on the contrary there never were two more lively, more agreable or more witty Girls, than we are; not an hour in the Day hangs heavy on our hands. We read, we work, we walk and when fatigued with these Employments releive our spirits, either by a lively song, a graceful Dance, or by some smart bon-mot, and witty repartée. We are handsome my dear Charlotte, very handsome and the greatest of our Perfections is, that we are entirely insensible of them ourselves. But why do I thus dwell on myself? Let me rather repeat the praise of our dear little Neice the innocent Louisa, who is at present sweetly smiling in a gentle Nap, as she reposes on the Sofa. The dear Creature is just turned of two years old; as handsome as tho' 2 & 20, as sensible as tho' 2 & 30, and as prudent as tho' 2 & 40. To convince you of this, I must inform you

---

[1] Rakehelly Dishonour Esqre.

that she has a very fine complexion and very pretty features, that she already knows the two first letters in the Alphabet, and that she never tears her frocks—. If I have not now convinced you of her Beauty, Sense & Prudence, I have nothing more to urge in support of my assertion, and you will therefore have no way of deciding the Affair but by coming to Lesley Castle, and by a personal acquaintance with Louisa, determine for yourself. Ah! my dear Freind, how happy should I be to see you within these venerable Walls! It is now four years since my removal from School has separated me from you; that two such tender Hearts, so closely linked together by the ties of simpathy and Freindship, should be so widely removed from each other, is vastly moving. I live in Perthshire, You in Sussex. We might meet in London, were my Father disposed to carry me there, and were your Mother to be there at the same time. We might meet at Bath, at Tunbridge, or anywhere else indeed, could we but be at the same place together. We have only to hope that such a period may arrive. My Father does not return to us till Autumn; my Brother will leave Scotland in a few Days; he is impatient to travel. Mistaken Youth! He vainly flatters himself that change of Air will heal the Wounds of a broken Heart! You will join with me I am certain my dear Charlotte, in prayers for the recovery of the unhappy Lesley's peace of Mind, which must ever be essential to that of your sincere freind

M. LESLEY.

Letter the second
From Miss C. Lutterell to Miss M. Lesley in answer

Glenford   Feb:ry 12

I HAVE a thousand excuses to beg for having so long delayed thanking you my dear Peggy for your agreable Letter, which beleive me I should not have deferred doing, had not every moment of my time during the last five weeks been so fully employed in the necessary arrangements for my sisters Wedding, as to allow me no time to devote either to you or myself. And now what provokes me more than anything else is that the Match is broke off, and all my Labour thrown away. Imagine how great the Disappointment must be to me, when you consider that after having laboured both by Night and Day, in order to get the Wedding dinner ready by the time appointed, after having roasted Beef, Broiled Mutton, and Stewed Soup enough to last the new-married Couple through the Honey-moon, I had the mortification of finding that I had been Roasting, Broiling and Stewing both the Meat and Myself to no purpose. Indeed my dear Freind, I never remember suffering any vexation equal to what I experienced on last Monday when my Sister came running to me in the Store-room with her face as White as a Whipt syllabub, and told me that Hervey had been thrown from his Horse, had fractured his Scull and was pronounced by his Surgeon to be in the most emminent Danger. "Good God! (said I) you dont say so? Why what in the name of Heaven will become of all the Victuals? We shall never be able to eat it while it is good. However, we'll call in the Surgeon to help us—. I shall be able to manage the Sir-loin myself; my Mother will eat the Soup, and You and the Doctor must finish the rest." Here I was interrupted, by seeing my poor Sister fall down to appearance Lifeless upon one of the Chests, where we keep our Table linen. I immediately called my Mother and the Maids, and at last we brought her to herself again; as soon as ever she was sensible, she expressed a determination of going instantly to Henry, and was so wildly bent on this Scheme, that we had the greatest Difficulty in the World to prevent her putting it in execution; at last however more by Force than Entreaty we prevailed on her to go into her room; we laid her upon the Bed, and she continued for some Hours in the most dreadful Convulsions. My Mother and I continued in the room with her, and when any intervals of tolerable Composure in Eloisa would allow us, we joined in heartfelt lamentations on the dreadful Waste in our provisions which this Event must occasion, and in concerting some plan for getting rid of them. We agreed that the best thing we could do was to begin eating them immediately, and accordingly we ordered up the cold Ham and Fowls, and instantly began our Devouring Plan on them with great Alacrity. We would have persuaded Eloisa to have taken a Wing of a Chicken, but she would not be persuaded. She was however much quieter than she had been; the Convulsions she had before suffered having given way to an almost perfect Insensibility. We endeavoured to rouse her by every means in our power, but to no purpose. I talked to her of Henry. "Dear Eloisa (said I) there's no occasion for your crying so much about such a trifle. (for I was willing to make light of it in order to comfort her) I beg you would not mind it—. You see it does not vex me in the least; though perhaps *I* may suffer most from it after all; for I shall not only be obliged to eat up all the Victuals I have dressed already, but must if Hervey should recover (which however is not very likely) dress as much for you again; or should he die (as I suppose he will) I shall still have to prepare a Dinner for you whenever you marry any one else. So you see that tho' perhaps for the present it may afflict you to think of Henry's sufferings, Yet I dare say he'll die soon, and then his pain will be over and you will be easy, whereas my Trouble will last much longer for work hard as I may, I am certain that the pantry cannot be cleared in less than a fortnight." Thus I did all in my power to console her, but without any effect, and at last as I saw that she did not seem to listen to me, I said no more, but leaving her with my Mother I took down the remains of The Ham & Chicken, and sent William to ask how Hervey did. He was not expected to live many Hours; he died the same day. We took all possible care to break the Melancholy Event to Eloisa in the tenderest manner; yet in spite of every precaution, her Sufferings on hearing it were too violent for her reason, and she continued for many hours in a high Delirium. She is still extremely ill, and her Physicians are greatly afraid of her going into a Decline. We are therefore preparing for Bristol, where we mean to be in the course of the next week. And now my dear Margaret let me talk a little of your affairs; and in the first place I must inform you that it is confidently reported, your Father is going to be married; I am very unwilling to beleive so unpleasing a report, and at the same time cannot wholly discredit it. I have written to my freind Susan Fitzgerald, for information concerning it, which as she is at present in Town, she will be very able to give me. I know not who is the Lady. I think your Brother is extremely right in the resolution he has taken of travelling, as it will perhaps contribute to obliterate from his remembrance, those disagreable Events, which have lately so much afflicted him—I am happy to find that tho' secluded from all the World, neither you nor Matilda are dull or unhappy—that you may never know what it is to be either is the wish of your sincerely Affectionate

C.L.

P.S. I have this instant received an answer from my freind Susan, which I enclose to you, and on which you will make your own reflections.

The enclosed Letter

My dear Charlotte

You could not have applied for information concerning the report of Sir George Lesleys Marriage, to anyone better able to give it you than I am. Sir George is certainly married; I was myself present at the Ceremony, which you will not be surprised at when I subscribe myself your

Affectionate
Susan Lesley

Letter the third
From Miss Margaret Lesley to Miss C. Lutterell

Lesley Castle   February the 16th

I *have* made my own reflections on the letter you enclosed to me, my Dear Charlotte and I will now tell you what those reflections were. I reflected that if by this second Marriage Sir George should have a second family, our fortunes must be considerably diminushed—that if his Wife should be of an extravagant turn, she would encourage him to persevere in that Gay & Dissipated way of Life to which little encouragement would be necessary, and which has I fear already proved but too detrimental to his health and fortune—that she would now become Mistress of those Jewels which once adorned our Mother, and which Sir George had always

promised us—that if they did not come into Perthshire I should not be able to
gratify my curiosity of beholding my Mother-in-law, and that if they did, Matilda
would no longer sit at the head of her Father's table—. These my dear Charlotte
were the melancholy reflections which crouded into my imagination after perusing Susan's letter to you, and which instantly occurred to Matilda when she had
perused it likewise. The same ideas, the same fears, immediately occupied her
Mind, and I know not which reflection distressed her most, whether the probable
Diminution of our Fortunes, or her own Consequence. We both wish very much
to know whether Lady Lesley is handsome & what is your opinion of her; as you
honour her with the appellation of your freind, we flatter ourselves that she must
be amiable. My Brother is already in Paris. He intends to quit it in a few Days,
and to begin his route to Italy. He writes in a most chearfull Manner, says that the
air of France has greatly recovered both his Health and Spirits; that he has now
entirely ceased to think of Louisa with any degree either of Pity or Affection, that
he even feels himself obliged to her for her Elopement, as he thinks it very good
fun to be single again. By this, you may perceive that he has entirely regained that
chearful Gaiety, and sprightly Wit, for which he was once so remarkable. When he
first became acquainted with Louisa which was little more than three years ago, he
was one of the most lively, the most agreable young Men of the age—. I beleive you
never yet heard the particulars of his first acquaintance with her. It commenced
at our cousin Colonel Drummond's, at whose house in Cumberland he spent the
Christmas, in which he attained the age of two and twenty. Louisa Burton was
the Daughter of a distant Relation of Mrs. Drummond, who dieing a few Months
before in extreme poverty, left his only Child then about eighteen to the protection
of any of his Relations who would protect her. Mrs. Drummond was the only one
who found herself so disposed—Louisa was therefore removed from a miserable
Cottage in Yorkshire to an elegant Mansion in Cumberland, and from every pecuniary Distress that Poverty could inflict, to every elegant Enjoyment that Money
could purchase—. Louisa was naturally ill-tempered and Cunning; but she had
been taught to disguise her real Disposition, under the appearance of insinuating
Sweetness by a father who but too well knew, that to be married, would be the only
chance she would have of not being starved, and who flattered himself that with
such an extraoidinary share of personal beauty, joined to a gentleness of Manners,
and an engaging address, she might stand a good chance of pleasing some young
Man who might afford to marry a Girl without a Shilling. Louisa perfectly entered
into her father's schemes and was determined to forward them with all her care &
attention. By dint of Perseverance and Application, she had at length so thoroughly
disguised her natural disposition under the mask of Innocence, and Softness, as to
impose upon every one who had not by a long and constant intimacy with her discovered her real Character. Such was Louisa when the hapless Lesley first beheld
her at Drummond-house. His heart which (to use your favourite comparison) was

as delicate as sweet and as tender as a Whipt-syllabub, could not resist her attractions. In a very few Days, he was falling in love, shortly afterwards actually fell, and before he had known her a Month, he had married her. My Father was at first highly displeased at so hasty and imprudent a connection; but when he found that they did not mind it, he soon became perfectly reconciled to the match. The Estate near Aberdeen which my brother possesses by the bounty of his great Uncle independant of Sir George, was entirely sufficient to support him and my Sister in Elegance & Ease. For the first twelvemonth, no one could be happier than Lesley, and no one more amiable to appearance than Louisa, and so plausibly did She act and so cautiously behave that tho' Matilda and I often spent several weeks together with them, yet we neither of us had any suspicion of her real Disposition. After the birth of Louisa however, which one would have thought would have strengthened her regard for Lesley, the mask she had so long supported was by degrees thrown aside, and as probably she then thought herself secure in the affection of her Husband (which did indeed appear if possible augmented by the birth of his Child) She seemed to take no pains to prevent that affection from ever diminishing. Our visits therefore to Dunbeath, were now less frequent and by far less agreable than they used to be. Our absence was however never either mentioned or lamented by Louisa who in the society of the young Danvers with whom she became acquainted at Aberdeen (he was at one of the Universities there,) felt infinitely happier than in that of Matilda and your freind, tho' there certainly never were pleasanter Girls than we are. You know the sad end of all Lesleys connubial happiness; I will not repeat it—. Adeiu my dear Charlotte; although I have not yet mentioned any thing of the matter, I hope you will do me the justice to believe that I *think* and *feel*, a great deal for your Sisters affliction. I do not doubt but that the healthy air of the Bristol downs, will intirely remove it, by crasing from her Mind the remembrance of Henry.

I am my dear Charlotte yrs ever

ML—.

Letter the fourth
From Miss C. Lutterell to Miss M. Lesley

Bristol February 27th

MY DEAR PEGGY

I HAVE but just received your letter, which being directed to Sussex while I was at Bristol was obliged to be forwarded to me here, & from some unaccountable Delay, has but this instant reached me—. I return you many thanks for the account it contains of Lesley's acquaintance, Love & Marriage with Louisa, which has not the less entertained me for having often been repeated to me before.

I have the satisfaction of informing you that we have every reason to imagine our pantry is by this time nearly cleared, as we left particular orders with the Servants to eat as hard as they possibly could, and to call in a couple of Chairwomen to assist them. We brought a cold Pigeon pye, a cold turkey, a cold tongue, and half a dozen Jellies with us, which we were lucky enough with the help of our Landlady, her husband, and their three children, to get rid of, in less than two days after our arrival. Poor Eloisa is still so very indifferent both in Health & Spirits, that I very much fear, the air of the Bristol downs, healthy as it is, has not been able to drive poor Henry from her remembrance.

You ask me whether your new Mother in law is handsome & amiable—I will now give you an exact description of her bodily and mental charms. She is short, and extremely well-made; is naturally pale, but rouges a good deal; has fine eyes, and fine teeth, as she will take care to let you know as soon as she sees you, and is altogether very pretty. She is remarkably good-tempered when she has her own way, and very lively when she is not out of humour. She is naturally extravagant and not very affected; she never reads anything but the letters she receives from me, and never writes anything but her answers to them. She plays, sings & Dances, but has no taste for either, and excells in none, tho' she says she is passionately fond of all. Perhaps you may flatter me so far as to be surprised that one of whom I speak with so little affection should be my particular freind; but to tell you the truth, our freindship arose rather from Caprice on her side than Esteem on mine. We spent two or three days together with a Lady in Berkshire with whom we both happened to be connected—. During our visit, the Weather being remarkably bad, and our party particularly stupid, she was so good as to conceive a violent partiality for me, which very soon settled in a downright Freindship, and ended in an established correspondence. She is probably by this time as tired of me, as I am of her; but as she is too polite and I am too civil to say so, our letters are still as frequent and affectionate as ever, and our Attachment as firm and sincere as when it first commenced.— As she had a great taste for the pleasures of London, and of Brighthelmstone, she will I dare say find some difficulty in prevailing on herself ever to satisfy the curiosity I dare say she feels of beholding you, at the expence of quitting those favourite haunts of Dissipation, for the melancholy tho' venerable gloom of the castle you inhabit. Perhaps however if she finds her health impaired by too much amusement, she may acquire fortitude sufficient to undertake a Journey to Scotland in the hope of its proving at least beneficial to her health, if not conducive to her happiness. Your fears I am sorry to say, concerning your fathers extravagance, your own fortunes, your Mothers Jewels and your Sister's consequence, I should suppose are but too well founded. My freind herself has four thousand pounds, and will probably spend nearly as much every year in Dress and Public places, if she can get it—she will certainly not endeavour to reclaim Sir George from the manner of living to which he has been so long accustomed, and there is therefore some reason to fear that you will be very well off, if you get any fortune at all. The Jewels I should imagine too will undoubtedly be hers, & there is too much reason to think that she will reside at her Husbands table in preference to his Daughter. But as so melancholy a subject must necessarily extremely distress you, I will no longer dwell on it—.

Eloisa's indisposition has brought us to Bristol at so unfashionable a season of the year, that we have actually seen but one genteel family since we came. Mr & Mrs Marlowe are very agreable people; the ill health of their little boy occasioned their arrival here; you may imagine that being the only family with whom we can converse, we are of course on a footing of intimacy with them; we see them indeed almost every day, and dined with them yesterday. We spent a very pleasant Day, and had a very good Dinner, tho' to be sure the Veal was terribly underdone, and the Curry had no seasoning. I could not help wishing all dinner-time that I had been at the dressing it—. A brother of Mrs Marlowe, Mr Cleveland is with them at present; he is a good-looking young Man, and seems to have a good deal to say for himself. I tell Eloisa that she should set her cap at him, but she does not at all seem to relish the proposal. I should like to see the girl married and Cleveland has a very good estate. Perhaps you may wonder that I do not consider *myself* as well as my Sister in my matrimonial Projects; but to tell you the truth I never wish to act a more principal part at a Wedding than the superintending and directing the Dinner, and therefore while I can get any of my acquaintance to marry for me, I shall never think of doing it myself, as I very much suspect that I should not have so much time for dressing my own Wedding-dinner, as for dressing that of my freinds.

Yrs sincerely
CL.

Letter the fifth
Miss Margaret Lesley to Miss Charlotte Lutterell

Lesley-Castle   March 18th

On the same day that I received your last kind letter, Matilda received one from Sir George which was dated from Edinburgh, and informed us that he should do himself the pleasure of introducing Lady Lesley to us on the following evening. This as you may suppose considerably surprised us, particularly as your account of her Ladyship had given us reason to imagine there was little chance of her visiting Scotland at a time that London must be so gay. As it was our business however to be delighted at such a mark of condescension as a visit from Sir George and Lady Lesley, we prepared to return them an answer expressive of the happiness we enjoyed in expectation of such a Blessing, when luckily recollecting that as they were to reach the Castle the next Evening, it would be impossible for my father to receive it before he left Edinburgh, We contented ourselves with leaving them to suppose that we were as happy as we ought to be. At nine in the Evening on the following day, they came, accompanied by one of Lady Lesleys brothers. Her Ladyship perfectly answers the description you sent me of her, except that I do not think her so pretty as you seem to consider her. She has not a bad face, but there is something so extremely unmajestic in her little diminutive figure, as to render her in comparison with the elegant height of Matilda and Myself, an insignificant Dwarf. Her curiosity to see us (which must have been great to bring her more than four hundred miles) being now perfectly gratified, she already begins to mention their return to town, and has desired us to accompany her—. We cannot refuse her request since it is seconded by the commands of our Father, and thirded by the entreaties of Mr Fitzgerald who is certainly one of the most pleasing young Men, I ever beheld, It is not yet determined when we are to go, but when ever we do we shall certainly take our little Louisa with us. Adeiu my dear Charlotte; Matilda unites in best Wishes to You & Eloisa, with your ever

M L

Letter the sixth
Lady Lesley to Miss Charlotte Lutterell

Lesley-Castle   March 20th

WE arrived here my sweet Freind about a fortnight ago, and I already heartily repent that I ever left our charming House in Portman-Square for such a dismal old weather-beaten Castle as this. You can form no idea sufficiently hideous, of its dungeon-like form. It is actually perched upon a Rock to appearance so totally inaccessible, that I expected to have been pulled up by a rope; and sincerely repented having gratified my curiosity to behold my Daughters at the expence of being obliged to enter their prison in so dangerous & ridiculous a Manner. But as soon as I once found myself safely arrived in the inside of this tremendous building, I comforted myself with the hope of having my spirits revived, by the sight of the two beautifull Girls, such as the Miss Lesleys had been represented to me, at Edinburgh. But here again, I met with nothing but Disapointment and Surprise. Matilda and Margaret Lesley are two great, tall, out of the way, over-grown Girls, just of a proper size to inhabit a Castle almost as Large in comparison as themselves. I wish my dear Charlotte that you could but behold these Scotch Giants;

I am sure they would frighten you out of your wits. They will do very well as foils to myself, so I have invited them to accompany me to London where I hope to be in the course of a fortnight. Besides these two fair Damsels, I found a little humoured Brat here who I believe is some relation to them; they told me who she was, and gave me a long rigmerole story of her father and Miss *Somebody* which I have entirely forgot. I hate Scandal and detest Children.—. I have been plagued ever since I came here with tiresome visits from a parcel of Scotch wretches, with terrible hard names; they were so civil, gave me so many invitations, and talked of coming again so soon, that I could not help affronting them. I suppose I shall not see them any more, and yet as a family party we are so stupid, that I do not know what to do with myself. These girls have no Music, but Scotch Airs, no Drawings but Scotch Mountains, and no Books but Scotch Poems—And I hate everything Scotch. In general I can spend half the Day at my toilett with a great deal of pleasure, but why should I dress here, since there is not a creature in the House whom I have any wish to please.—. I have just had a conversation with my Brother in which he has greatly offended me, and which as I have nothing more entertaining to send you I will give you the particulars of. You must know that I have for these 4 or 5 Days past strongly suspected William of entertaining a partiality to my eldest Daughter. I own indeed that had *I* been inclined to fall in love with any woman, I should not have made choice of Matilda Lesley for the object of my passion; for there is nothing I hate so much as a tall Woman: but however there is no accounting for some men's taste and as William is himself nearly six feet high, it is not wonderful that he should be partial to that height. Now as I have a very great Affection for my Brother and should be extremely sorry to see him unhappy, which I suppose he means to be if he cannot marry Matilda, as moreover I know that his Circumstances will not allow him to marry any one without a fortune, and that Matilda's is entirely dependant on her Father, who will neither have his own inclination, nor my permission to give her anything at present, I thought it would be doing a good-natured action by my Brother to let him know as much, in order that he might choose for himself, whether to conquer his passion, or Love and Despair. Accordingly finding myself this Morning alone with him in one of the horrid old rooms of this Castle, I opened the cause to him in the following Manner.

"Well my dear William what do you think of these girls? for my part, I do not find them so plain as I expected; but perhaps you may think me partial to the Daughters of my Husband and perhaps you are right—They are indeed so very like Sir George that it is natural to think. ."....

"My Dear Susan (cried he in a tone of the greatest amazement) You do not really think they bear the least resemblance to their Father! He is so very plain!— but I beg your pardon—I had entirely forgotten to whom I was speaking—"

"Oh! pray dont mind me; (replied I) every one knows Sir George is horribly ugly, and I assure you I always thought him a fright."

"You surprise me extremely (answered William) by what you say both with respect to Sir George and his daughters. You cannot think your Husband so deficient in personal Charms as you speak of, nor can you surely see any resemblance between him and the Miss Lesleys who are in my opinion perfectly unlike him & perfectly Handsome."

"If that is your opinion with regard to the Girls it certainly is no proof of their Fathers beauty, for if they are perfectly unlike him and very handsome at the same time, it is natural to suppose that he is very plain."

"By no means, (said he) for what may be pretty in a Woman, may be very unpleasing in a Man."

"But you yourself (replied I) but a few Minutes ago allowed him to be very plain."

"Men are no Judges of Beauty in their own Sex." (said he)

"Neither Men nor Women can think Sir George tolerable."

"Well, well, (said he) we will not dispute about *his* Beauty, but your opinion of his *Daughters* is surely very singular, for if I understood you right, you said you did not find them so plain as you expected to do."!

"Why, do *you* find them plainer then?" (said I).

"I can scarcely beleive you to be serious (returned he) when you speak of their persons in so extroidinary a Manner. Do not you think the Miss Lesleys are two very handsome young Women?"

"Lord! No! (cried I) I think them terribly plain!"

"Plain! (replied He) My dear Susan, you cannot really think so! why what single Feature in the face of either of them, can you possibly find fault with?"

"Oh! trust me for that; (replied I). Come I will begin with the eldest—with Matilda. Shall I, William? (I looked as cunning as I could when I said it, in order to shame him.)

"They are so much alike (said he) that I should suppose the faults of one, would be the faults of both."

"Well, then, in the first place, they are both so horribly tall!"

"They are *taller* than you are indeed." (said he with a saucy smile).

"Nay, (said I); I know nothing of that."

"Well, but (he continued) tho' they may be above the common size, their figures are perfectly elegant; and as to their faces, their Eyes are beautifull—."

"I can never think such tremendous knock-me-down figures in the least degree elegant, and as for their eyes, they are so tall that I never could strain my neck enough to look at them."

"Nay, (replied he), I know not whether you may not be in the right in not attempting it, for perhaps they might dazzle you with their Lustre."

"Oh! Certainly." (said I, with the greatest Complacency, for I assure you my dearest Charlotte I was not in the least offended tho' by what followed, one would suppose that William was conscious of having given me just cause to be so, for coming up to me and taking my hand, he said) "You must not look so grave Susan; you will make me fear I have offended you!"

"Offended me! Dear Brother, how came such a thought in your head! (returned I) No really! I assure you that I am not in the least surprised at your being so warm an advocate for the Beauty of these girls"—

"Well, but (interrupted William) remember that we have not yet concluded our dispute concerning them. What fault do you find with their complexion?"

"They are so horribly pale."

"They always have a little colour, and after any exercise it is considerably heightened."

"Yes, but if there should ever happen to be any rain in this part of the world, they will never be able to raise more than their common stock—except indeed they amuse themselves with running up & Down these horrid Galleries and Antichambers—"

"Well, (replied my Brother in a tone of vexation, & glancing an impertinent Look at me) if they *have* but little colour, at least, it is all their own."

This was too much my dear Charlotte, for I am certain that he had the impudence by that look, of pretending to suspect the reality of mine. But you I am sure will indicate my character whenever you may hear it so cruelly aspersed, for you can witness how often I have protested against wearing Rouge, and how much I always told you I dislike it. And I assure you that my opinions are still the same.—. Well, not bearing to be so suspected by my Brother, I left the room immediately, and have ever since been in my own Dressing-room writing to you. What a long Letter have I made of it! But you must not expect to receive such from me when I get to Town; for it is only at Lesley castle, that one has time to write even to a Charlotte Lutterell.—. I was so much vexed by William's Glance, that I could not summon Patience enough, to stay & give him that Advice respecting his Attachment to Matilda which had first induced me from pure Love to him to begin the conversation; and I am now so thoroughly convinced by it, of his violent passion for her, that I am certain he would never hear reason on the Subject, and I shall therefore give myself no more trouble either about him or his favourite.

Adeiu my dear Girl—
Yrs Affectionately Susan L.

Letter the seventh
From Miss C. Lutterell to Miss M. Lesley

Bristol the 27th of March.

I HAVE received Letters from You & your Mother-in-Law within this week which have greatly entertained me, as I find by them that you are both downright jealous of each others Beauty. It is very odd that two pretty Women tho' actually Mother & Daughter cannot be in the same House without falling out about their faces. Do be convinced that you are both perfectly handsome and say no more of the Matter. I suppose this Letter must be directed to Portman Square where probably (great as is your affection for Lesley Castle) you will not be sorry to find yourself. In spite of all that People may say about Green fields and the Country I was always of the opinion that London and its Amusements must be very agreable for a while, and should be very happy could my Mother's income allow her to jockey us into its Public-places, during Winter. I always longed particularly to go to Vaux-hall, to see whether the cold Beef there is cut so thin as it is reported, for I have a sly suspicion that few people understand the art of cutting a slice of cold Beef so well as I do: nay it would be hard if I did not know something of the Matter, for it was a part of my Education that I took by far the most pains with. Mama always found me *her* best Scholar, tho' when Papa was alive Eloisa was *his*. Never to be sure were there two more different Dispositions in the World. We both loved Reading. *She* preferred Histories, & *I* Receipts. She loved drawing Pictures, and I drawing Pullets. No one could sing a better Song than She, and no one make a better Pye than I.—And so it has always continued since we have been no longer Children. The only difference is that all disputes on the superior excellence of our Employments *then* so frequent are now no more. We have for many years entered into an agreement always to admire each other's works; I never fail listening to *her* Music, & she is as constant in eating *my* pies. Such at least was the case till Henry Hervey made his appearance in Sussex. Before the arrival of his Aunt in our neighourhood where she established herself you know about a twelvemonth ago, his visits to her had been at stated times, and of equal & settled Duration; but on her removal to the Hall which is within a walk from our House, they became both more frequent & longer. This as you may suppose could not be pleasing to Mrs Diana who is a professed Enemy to everything which is not directed by Decorum and Formality, or which bears the least resemblance to Ease and Good-breeding. Nay so great was her aversion to her Nephews behaviour that I have often heard her give such hints of it before his face that had not Henry at such times been engaged in conversation with Eloisa, they must have caught his Attention and have very much distressed him. The alteration in my Sisters behaviour which I have before hinted at, now took place. The Agreement we had entered into of admiring each others productions she no longer seemed to regard & tho' I constantly applauded even every Country-dance, She play'd, yet not even a pidgeon-pye of my making could obtain from her a single word of approbation. This was certainly enough to put any one in a Passion; however, I was as cool as a Cream-cheese and having formed my plan & concerted a scheme of Revenge, I was determined to let her have her own way & not even to make her a single reproach. My Scheme was to treat her as she treated me, and tho' she might even draw my own Picture or play Malbrook (which is the only tune I ever really like) not to say so much as "Thank you Eloisa;" tho' I had for many years constantly hollowed whenever she played, *Bravo, Bravissimo, Encora, Da Capo, allegretto, con expressione,* and *Poco presto* with many other such outlandish words, all of them as Eloisa told me expressive of my Admiration; and so indeed I suppose they are, as I see some of them in every Page of every Music book, being the Sentiments I imagine of the Composer.

I executed my Plan with great Punctuality; I can not say success, for Alas! my silence while she played seemed not in the least to displease her; on the contrary she actually said to me one day "Well Charlotte, I am very glad to find that you have at last left off that ridiculous custom of applauding my Execution on the Harpsichord till you made *my* head ake, & yourself hoarse. I feel very much obliged to you for keeping your Admiration to yourself." I never shall forget the very witty answer I made to this speech. "Eloisa (said I) I beg you would be quite at your Ease with respect to all such fears in future, for be assured that I shall always keep my Admiration to myself, & my own pursuits & never extend it to yours." This was the only very severe thing I ever said in my Life; not but that I have often felt myself extremely satirical but it was the only time I ever made my feelings public.

I suppose there never were two young people who had a greater affection for each other than Henry & Eloisa; no, the Love of your Brother for Miss Burton could not be so strong tho' it might be more violent. You may imagine therefore how provoked my Sister must have been to have him play her such a trick. Poor Girl! she still laments his Death with undiminished Constancy, notwithstanding he has been dead more than six weeks; but some people mind such things more than others. The ill state of Health into which his Loss has thrown her makes her so weak, & so unable to support the least exertion, that she has been in tears all this Morning merely from having taken Leave of Mrs Marlowe who with Her husband, Brother and Child are to leave Bristol this Morning. I am sorry to have them go because they are the only family with whom we have here any acquaintance, but I never thought of crying; to be sure Eloisa & Mrs Marlowe have always been more together than with me, and have therefore contracted a kind of affection for each other, which does not make Tears so inexcusable in them as they would be in me. The Marlowes are going to Town; Cleveland accompanies them; as neither Eloisa nor I could catch him I hope you or Matilda may have better Luck. I know not when we shall leave Bristol, Eloisa's Spirits are so low that she is very averse to moving, and yet is certainly by no means mended by her residence here. A week or two will I hope determine our Measures—in the mean time believe me

&c—&c—CHARLOTTE LUTTERELL

Letter the Eighth
Miss Lutterell to Mrs Marlowe

Bristol   April 4th

I FEEL myself greatly obliged to you my dear Emma for such a mark of your affection as I flatter myself was conveyed in the proposal you made me of our Corresponding; I assure you that it will be a great releif to me to write to you and as long as my Health & Spirits will allow me, you will find me a very constant Correspondent; I will not say an entertaining one, for you know my situation sufficiently not to be ignorant that in me Mirth would be improper & I know my own Heart too well not to be sensible that it would be unnatural. You must not expect News for we see no one with whom we are in the least acquainted, or in whose proceedings we have any Interest. You must not expect Scandal for by the same rule we are equally debarred either from hearing or inventing it.—You must expect from me nothing but the melancholy effusions of a broken Heart which is ever reverting to the Happiness it once enjoyed and which ill supports its present wretchedness. The Possibility of being able to write, to speak, to you, of my lost Henry will be a Luxury to me, & your Goodness will not I know refuse to read what it will so much releive my Heart to write. I once thought that to have what is in general called a Freind (I mean one of my own Sex to whom I might speak with less reserve than to any other person) independant of my Sister would never be an object of my wishes, but how much was I mistaken! Charlotte is too much engrossed by two confidential Correspondents of that sort, to supply the place of one to me, & I hope you will not think me girlishly romantic, when I say that to have some kind and compassionate Freind who might listen to my Sorrows without endeavouring to console me was what I had for some time wished for, when our acquaintance with you, the intimacy which followed it & the particular affectionate Attention you paid me almost from the first, caused me to entertain the flattering Idea of those attentions being improved on a closer acquaintance into a Freindship which, if you were what my wishes formed you would be the greatest Happiness I could be capable of enjoying. To find that such Hopes are realised is a satisfaction indeed, a satisfaction which is now almost the only one I can ever experience.—I feel myself so languid that I am sure were you with me you would oblige me to leave off writing, & I cannot give you a greater proof of my Affection for you than by acting as I know you would wish me to do, whether Absent or Present. I am my dear Emmas sincere freind

E.L.

Letter the Ninth
Mrs Marlowe to Miss Lutterell

Grosvenor Street, April 10th

NEED I say my dear Eloisa how wellcome your Letter was to me? I cannot give a greater proof of the pleasure I received from it, or of the Desire I feel that our Correspondence may be regular & frequent than by setting you so good an example as I now do in answering it before the end of the week—. But do not imagine that I claim any merit in being so punctual; on the contrary I assure you, that it is a far greater Gratification to me to write to you, than to spend the Evening either at a Concert or a Ball. Mr Marlowe is so desirous of my appearing at some of the Public places every evening that I do not like to refuse him, but at the same time so much wish to remain at Home, that independant of the Pleasure I experience in devoting any portion of my Time to my Dear Eloisa, yet the Liberty I claim from having a Letter to write of spending an Evening at home with my little Boy, You know me well enough to be sensible, will of itself be a sufficient Inducement (if one is necessary) to my maintaining with Pleasure a Correspondence with you. As to the Subjects of your Letters to me, whether Grave or Merry, if they concern you they must be equally interesting to me; Not but that I think the Melancholy Indulgence of your own Sorrows by repeating them & dwelling on them to me, will only encourage and increase them, and that it will be more prudent in you to avoid so sad a subject; but yet knowing as I do what a soothing & Melancholy Pleasure it must afford you, I cannot prevail on myself to deny you so great an Indulgence, and will only insist on your not expecting me to encourage you in it, by my own Letters; on the contrary I intend to fill them with such lively Wit and enlivening Humour as shall even provoke a Smile in the sweet but sorrowfull Countenance of my Eloisa.

In the first place you are to learn that I have met your Sisters three freinds Lady Lesley and her Daughters, twice in Public since I have been here. I know you will be impatient to hear my opinion of the Beauty of three Ladies of whom You have heard so much. Now, as you are too ill & too unhappy to be vain, I think I may venture to inform you that I like none of their faces so well as I do your own. Yet they are all handsome—Lady Lesley indeed I have seen before; her Daughters I beleive would in general be said to have a finer face than her Ladyship, and Yet what with the charms of a Blooming Complexion, a little Affectation and a great deal of Small-talk, (in each of which She is superior to the Young Ladies) she will I dare say gain herself as many Admirers as the more regular features of Matilda, & Margaret. I am sure you will agree with me in saying that they can none of them be of a proper size for real Beauty, when you know that two of them are taller & the other shorter than ourselves. In spite of this Defect (or rather by reason of it) there is something very noble & majestic in the figures of the Miss Lesleys, and something agreably Lively in the Appearance of their pretty little Mother-in-law. But tho' one may be majestic & the other Lively, yet the faces of neither possess that Bewitching Sweetness of my Eloisas, which her present Languor is so far from diminushing. What would my Husband and Brother say of us, if they knew all the fine things I have been saying to you in this Letter. It is very hard that a pretty Woman is never to be told she is so by any one of her own Sex, without that person's being suspected to be either her determined Enemy, or her professed Toad-eater. How much more amiable are women in that particular! one man may say forty civil things to another without our supposing that he is ever paid for it, and provided he does his Duty by our Sex, we care not how Polite he is to his own.

    Mrs Lutterell will be so good as to accept my Compliments, Charlotte, my Love, and Eloisa the best wishes for the recovery of her Health & Spirits that can be offered by her Affectionate Freind

E.MARLOWE

I am afraid this Letter will be but a poor Specimen of my Powers in the Witty Way; and your opinion of them will not be greatly increased when I assure you that I have been as entertaining as I possibly could—.

Letter the Tenth
From Miss Margaret Lesley to Miss Charlotte Lutterell

Portman Square   April 13th

My dear Charlotte

We left Lesley-Castle on the 28th of Last Month, and arrived Safely in London after a Journey of seven Days; I had the pleasure of finding your Letter here waiting my Arrival, for which you have my grateful Thanks. Ah! my dear Freind I every day more regret the serene and tranquil Pleasures of the Castle we have left, in exchange for the uncertain & unequal Amusements of this vaunted City. Not that I will pretend to assert that these uncertain and unequal Amusements are in the least Degree unpleasing to me; on the contrary I enjoy them extremely and should enjoy them even more, were I not certain that every appearance I make in Public but rivetts the Chains of those unhappy Beings whose Passion it is impossible not to pity, tho' it is out of my power to return. In short my Dear Charlotte it is my sensibility for the sufferings of so many amiable Young Men, my Dislike of the extreme Admiration I meet with, and my Aversion to being so celebrated both in Public, in Private, in Papers, & in Printshops, that are the reasons why I cannot more fully enjoy, the Amusements so various and pleasing of London. How often have I wished that I possessed as little personal Beauty as you do; that my figure were as inelegant; my face as unlovely; and my Appearance as unpleasing as yours! But ah! what little chance is there of so desirable an Event; I have had the Small-pox, and must therefore submit to my unhappy fate.

I am now going to intrust you my dear Charlotte with a secret which has long disturbed the tranquillity of my days, and which is of a kind to require the most inviolable Secrecy from you. Last Monday se'night Matilda & I accompanied Lady Lesley to a Rout at the Honourable Mrs Kickabout's; we were escorted by Mr Fitzgerald who is a very amiable Young Man in the main, tho' perhaps a little singular in his Taste—He is in love with Matilda—We had scarcely paid our Compliments to the Lady of the House and curtseyed to half a Score different people when my Attention was attracted by the appearance of a Young Man the most lovely of his Sex, who at that moment entered the Room with another Gentleman & Lady. From the first moment I beheld him, I was certain that on him depended the future Happiness of my Life. Imagine my surprise when he was introduced to me by the name of Cleveland—I instantly recognised him as the Brother of Mrs Marlowe, and the acquaintance of my Charlotte at Bristol. Mr and Mrs M. were the gentleman & Lady who accompanied him. (You do not think Mrs Marlowe handsome?) The elegant address of Mr Cleveland, his polished Manners and Delightful Bow, at once confirmed my attachment. He did not speak; but I can imagine every thing he would have said, had he opened his Mouth. I can picture to myself the cultivated Understanding, the Noble Sentiments, & elegant Language which would have shone so conspicuous in the conversation of Mr Cleveland. The approach of Sir James Gower (one of my too numerous Admirers) prevented the Discovery of any such Powers, by putting an end to a conversation we had never commenced, and by attracting my attention to himself. But oh! how inferior are the accomplishments of Sir James to those of his so greatly envied Rival! Sir James is one of the most frequent of our Visitors, & is almost always of our Parties. We have since often met Mr & Mrs Marlowe but no Cleveland—he is always engaged some where else. Mrs Marlowe fatigues me to Death every time I see her by her tiresome conversations about You & Eloisa. She is so Stupid! I live in the hope of seeing her irrisistable Brother to night, as we are going to Lady Flambeau's, who is I know intimate with the Marlowes. Our party will be Lady Lesley, Matilda, Fitzgerald, Sir James Gower, & myself. We see little of Sir George, who is almost always at the Gaming-table. Ah! my poor Fortune, where art thou by this time? We see more of Lady L. who always makes her appearance (highly rouged) at Dinner-time. Alas! what Delightful Jewels will she be decked in this evening at Lady Flambeau's!; Yet I wonder how she can herself delight in wearing them; surely she must be sensible of the ridiculous impropriety of loading her little diminutive figure with such superfluous ornaments; is it possible that she can not know how greatly superior an elegant simplicity is to the most studied apparel? Would she but present them to Matilda & me, how greatly should we be obliged to her. How becoming would Diamonds be on our fine majestic figures! And how surprising it is that such an Idea should never have occurred to *her*. I am sure if I have reflected in this Manner once, I have fifty times. Whenever I see Lady Lesley dressed in them such reflections immediately come across me. My own Mother's Jewels too! But I will say no more on so melancholy a Subject—Let me entertain you with something more pleasing—Matilda had a letter this Morning from Lesley, by which we have the pleasure of finding he is at Naples has turned Roman-catholic, obtained one of the Pope's Bulls for annulling his 1st Marriage and had since actually married a Neapolitan Lady of great Rank & Fortune. He tells us moreover that much the same sort of affair has befallen his first wife the worthless Louisa who is likewise at Naples has turned Roman-catholic, and is soon to be married to a Neapolitan Nobleman of great & Distinguished Merit. He says, that they are at present very good Freinds, have quite forgiven all past errors and intend in future to be very good Neighbours. He invites Matilda & me to pay him a visit in Italy and to bring him his little Louisa whom both her Mother, Step-Mother, and himself are equally desirous of beholding. As to our accepting his invitation, it is at present very uncertain; Lady Lesley advises us to go without loss of time; Fitzgerald offers to escort us there, but Matilda has some doubts of the Propriety of such a Scheme—She owns it would be very agreable. I am certain she likes the Fellow. My Father desires us not to be in a hurry, as perhaps if we wait a few months both he & Lady Lesley will do themselves the pleasure of attending us. Lady Lesley says no, that nothing will ever tempt her to forego the Amusements of Brighthelmstone for a Journey to Italy merely to see our Brother. "No (says the disagreable woman) I have once in my life been fool enough to travel I dont know how many hundred Miles to see two of the Family, and I found it did not answer, so Deuce take me, if ever I am so foolish again." So says her Ladyship, but Sir George still perseveres in saying that perhaps in a Month or two, they may accompany us.

Adeiu my Dear Charlotte—
YR FAITHFUL MARGARET LESLEY

The History of England from the reign of
Henry the 4th to the death of Charles the 1st

By a partial, prejudiced, & ignorant Historian. To Miss Austen eldest daughter of the Revd George Austen, this Work is inscribed with all due respect by

THE AUTHOR

N.B. There will be very few Dates in this History.

HENRY THE 4TH

HENRY the 4th ascended the throne of England much to his own satisfaction in the year 1399, after having prevailed on his cousin & predecessor Richard the 2d, to resign it to him, & to retire for the rest of his Life to Pomfret Castle, where he happened to be murdered. It is to be supposed that Henry was married, since he had certainly four sons, but it is not in my power to inform the Reader who was his Wife. Be this as it may, he did not live for ever, but falling ill, his son the Prince of Wales came and took away the crown; whereupon the King made a long speech, for which I must refer the Reader to Shakespear's Plays, & the Prince made a still longer. Things being thus settled between them the King died, & was succeeded by his son Henry who had previously beat Sir William Gascoigne.

HENRY THE 5TH

THIS Prince after he succeeded to the throne grew quite reformed & Amiable, forsaking all his dissipated Companions, & never thrashing Sir William again. During his reign, Lord Cobham was burnt alive, but I forget what for. His Majesty then turned his thoughts to France, where he went & fought the famous Battle of Agincourt. He afterwards married the King's daughter Catherine, a very agreable Woman by Shakespear's account. In spite of all this however he died, and was succeeded by his son Henry.

HENRY THE 6TH

I CANNOT say much for this Monarch's Sense—Nor would I if I could, for he was a Lancastrian. I suppose you know all about the Wars between him & The Duke of York who was of the right side; If you do not, you had better read some other History, for I shall not be very diffuse in this, meaning by it only to vent my Spleen *against*, & shew my Hatred *to* all those people whose parties or principles do not suit with mine, & not to give information. This King married Margaret of Anjou, a Woman whose distresses & Misfortunes were so great as almost to make me who hate her, pity her. It was in this reign that Joan of Arc lived & made such a *row* among the English. They should not have burnt her—but they did. There were several Battles between the Yorkists & Lancastrians, in which the former (as they ought) usually conquered. At length they were entirely over come; The King was murdered—The Queen was sent home—& Edward the 4th Ascended the Throne.

EDWARD THE 4TH

THIS Monarch was famous only for his Beauty & his Courage, of which the Picture we have here given of him, & his undaunted Behaviour in marrying one Woman while he was engaged to another, are sufficient proofs. His wife was Elizabeth Woodville, a Widow, who, poor Woman!, was afterwards confined in a Convent by that Monster of Iniquity & Avarice Henry the 7th. One of Edward's Mistresses was Jane Shore, who has had a play written about her, but it is a tragedy & therefore not worth reading. Having performed all these noble actions, his Majesty died, & was succeeded by his Son.

EDWARD THE 5TH

THIS unfortunate Prince lived so little a while that no body had time to draw his picture. He was murdered by his Uncle's Contrivance, whose name was Richard the 3d.

RICHARD THE 3RD

THE Character of this Prince has been in general very severely treated by Historians, but as he was *York,* I am rather inclined to suppose him a very respectable Man. It has indeed been confidently asserted that he killed his two Nephews & his Wife, but it has also been declared that he did *not* kill his two Nephews, which I am inclined to beleive true; & if this is the case, it may also be affirmed that he did not kill his Wife, for if Perkin Warbeck was really the Duke of York, why might not Lambert Simnel be the Widow of Richard. Whether innocent or guilty, he did not reign long in peace, for Henry Tudor E. of Richmond as great a Villain as ever lived, made a great fuss about getting the Crown & having killed the King at the battle of Bosworth, he succeeded to it.

HENRY THE 7TH

THIS Monarch soon after his accession married the Princess Elizabeth of York, by which alliance he plainly proved that he thought his own right inferior to hers, tho' he pretended to the contrary. By this Marriage he had two sons & two daughters, the elder of which daughters was married to the King of Scotland & had the happiness of being grandmother to one of the first Characters in the World. But of *her*, I shall have occasion to speak more at large in future. The Youngest, Mary, married first the King of France & secondly the D. of Suffolk, by whom she had one daughter, afterwards the Mother of Lady Jane Grey, who tho' inferior to her lovely Cousin the Queen of Scots, was yet an amiable young woman and famous for reading Greek while other people were hunting. It was in the reign of Henry the 7th that Perkin Warbeck & Lambert Simnel before mentioned made their appearance, the former of whom was set in the Stocks, took shelter in Beaulieu Abbey, & was beheaded with the Earl of Warwick, & the latter was taken into the King's Kitchen. His Majesty died, & was succeeded by his son Henry whose only merit was his not being *quite* so bad as his daughter Elizabeth.

HENRY THE 8TH

It would be an affront to my Readers were I to suppose that they were not as well acquainted with the particulars of this King's reign as I am myself. It will therefore be saving *them* the task of reading again what they have read before, & *myself* the trouble of writing what I do not perfectly recollect, by giving only a slight sketch of the principal Events which marked his reign. Among these may be ranked Cardinal Wolsey's telling the father Abbott of Leicester Abbey that "he was come to lay his bones among them", the reformation in Religion, & the King's riding through the Streets of London with Anna Bullen. It is however but Justice, & my Duty to declare that this amiable Woman was entirely innocent of the Crimes with which she was accused, of which her Beauty, her Elegance, & her Sprightliness were sufficient proofs, not to mention her solemn protestations of Innocence, the weakness of the Charges against her, and the king's Character; all of which add some confirmation, tho' perhaps but slight ones when in comparison with those before alledged in her favour. Tho' I do not profess giving many dates, yet as I think it proper to give some & shall of course make choice of those which it is most necessary for the Reader to know, I think it right to inform him that her letter to the King was dated on the 6th of May. The Crimes & Cruelties of this Prince, were too numerous to be mentioned, (as this history I trust has fully shown;) & nothing can be said in his vindication, but that his abolishing Religious Houses & leaving them to the ruinous depredations of time has been of infinite use to the landscape of England in general, which probably was a principal motive for his doing it, since otherwise why should a Man who was of no Religion himself be at so much trouble to abolish one which had for Ages been established in the Kingdom. His Majesty's 5th wife was the Duke of Norfolk's Neice who, tho' universally acquitted of the crimes for which she was beheaded, has been by many people supposed to have led an abandoned Life before her Marriage—of this however I have many doubts, since she was a relation of that noble Duke of Norfolk who was so warm in the Queen of Scotland's cause, & who at last fell a victim to it. The king's last wife contrived to survive him, but with difficulty effected it. He was succeeded by his only son Edward.

EDWARD THE 6TH

As this prince was only nine years old at the time of his Father's death, he was considered by many people as too young to govern, & the late King happening to be of the same opinion, his mother's Brother the Duke of Somerset was chosen Protector of the realm during his minority. This Man was on the whole of a very amiable Character, & is somewhat of a favourite with me, tho' I would by no means pretend to affirm that he was equal to those first of Men Robert Earl of Essex, Delamere, or Gilpin. He was beheaded, of which he might with reason have been proud, had he known that such was the death of Mary Queen of Scotland; but as it was impossible that He should be conscious of what had never happened, it does not appear that he felt particularly delighted with the manner of it. After his decease the Duke of Northumberland had the care of the King & the Kingdom, & performed his trust of both so well that the King died & the Kingdom was left to his daughter in law the Lady Jane Grey, who has been already mentioned as reading Greek. Whether she really understood that language or whether such a Study proceeded only from an excess of vanity for which I beleive she was always rather remarkable, is uncertain. Whatever might be the cause, she preserved the same appearance of knowledge, & contempt of what was generally esteemed pleasure, during the whole of her Life, for she declared herself displeased with being appointed Queen, and while conducting to the Scaffold, she wrote a Sentence in Latin & another in Greek on seeing the dead Body of her Husband accidentally passing that way.

MARY

This Woman had the good luck of being advanced to the throne of England, inspite of the superior pretensions, Merit, & *Beauty* of her Cousins Mary Queen of Scotland & Jane Grey. Nor can I pity the Kingdom for the misfortunes they experienced during her Reign, since they fully deserved them, for having allowed her to succeed her Brother—which was a double peice of folly, since they might have foreseen that as she died without Children, she would be succeeded by that disgrace to humanity, that pest of society, Elizabeth. Many were the people who fell Martyrs to the Protestant Religion during her reign; I suppose not fewer than a dozen. She married Philip King of Spain who in her Sister's reign was famous for building Armadas. She died without issue, & then the dreadful moment came in which the destroyer of all comfort, the deceitful Betrayer of trust reposed in her, & the Murderess of her Cousin succeeded to the Throne.

ELIZABETH

It was the peculiar Misfortune of this Woman to have bad Ministers—Since wicked as she herself was, she could not have committed such extensive mischeif, had not these vile & abandoned men connived at, & encouraged her in her crimes. I know that it has by many people been asserted & beleived that Lord Burleigh, Sir Francis Walsingham, & the rest of those who filled the cheif offices of State were deserving, experienced, & able Ministers. But oh! how blinded such Writers & such Readers must be to true Merit, to Merit despised, neglected & defamed, if they can persist in such opinions when they reflect that these Men, these boasted Men were such Scandals to their Country & their Sex as to allow & assist their Queen in confining for the space of nineteen years, a *Woman* who if the claims of Relationship & Merit were no avail, yet as a Queen & as one who condescended to place confidence in her, had every reason to expect Assistance & Protection; and at length in allowing Elizabeth to bring this amiable Woman to an untimely, unmerited, and scandalous Death. Can any one if he reflects but for a moment on this blot, this everlasting blot upon their Understanding & their Character, allow any praise to Lord Burleigh or Sir Francis Walsingham? Oh! what must this bewitching Princess whose only freind was then the Duke of Norfolk, and whose only ones are now Mr Whitaker, Mrs Lefroy, Mrs Knight & myself, who was abandoned by her son, confined by her Cousin, Abused, reproached & villified by all, what must not her most noble mind have suffered when informed that Elizabeth had given orders for her Death! Yet she bore it with a most unshaken fortitude; firm in her Mind; Constant in her Religion; & prepared herself to meet the cruel fate to which she was doomed, with a magnanimity that could alone proceed from conscious Innocence. And yet could you Reader have beleived it possible that some hardened & zealous Protestants have even abused her for that Steadfastness in the Catholic Religion which reflected on her so much credit? But this is a striking proof of *their* narrow Souls & prejudiced Judgements who accuse her. She was executed in the Great Hall at Fortheringay Castle (sacred Place!) on Wednesday the 8th of February 1586—to the everlasting Reproach of Elizabeth, her Ministers, and of England in general. It may not be unnecessary before I entirely conclude my account of this ill-fated Queen, to observe that she had been accused of several crimes during the time of her reigning in Scotland, of which I now most seriously do assure my Reader that she was entirely innocent; having never been guilty of anything more than Imprudencies into which she was betrayed by the openness of her Heart, her Youth, & her Education. Having I trust by this assurance entirely done away every Suspicion & every doubt which might have arisen in the Reader's mind, from what other Historians have written of her, I shall proceed to mention the remaining Events that marked Elizabeth's reign. It was about this time that Sir Francis Drake the first English Navigator who sailed round the World, lived, to be the ornament of his Country & his profession. Yet great as he was, & justly celebrated as a Sailor, I cannot help foreseeing that he will be equalled in this or the next Century by one who tho' now but young, already promises to answer all the ardent & sanguine expectations of his Relations & Freinds, amongst whom I may class the amiable Lady to whom this work is dedicated, & my no less amiable Self.

Though of a different profession, and shining in a different Sphere of Life, yet equally conspicuous in the Character of an *Earl,* as Drake was in that of a *Sailor,* was Robert Devereux Lord Essex. This unfortunate young Man was not unlike in Character to that equally unfortunate one *Frederic Delamere.* The simile may be carried still farther, & Elizabeth the torment of Essex may be compared to the Emmeline of Delamere. It would be endless to recount the misfortunes of this noble & gallant Earl. It is sufficient to say that he was beheaded on the 25th of Febry, after having been Lord Leuitenant of Ireland, after having clapped his hand on his sword, and after performing many other services to his Country. Elizabeth did not long survive his loss, & died *so* miserable that were it not an injury to the memory of Mary I should pity her.

JAMES THE 1ST

THOUGH this King had some faults, among which & as the most principal, was his allowing his Mother's death, yet considered on the whole I cannot help liking him. He married Anne of Denmark, and had several Children; fortunately for him his eldest son Prince Henry died before his father or he might have experienced the evils which befell his unfortunate Brother.

As I am myself partial to the roman catholic religion, it is with infinite regret that I am obliged to blame the Behaviour of any Member of it; yet Truth being I think very excusable in an Historian, I am necessitated to say that in this reign the roman Catholics of England did not behave like Gentlemen to the protestants. Their Behaviour indeed to the Royal Family & both Houses of Parliament might justly be considered by them as very uncivil, and even Sir Henry Percy tho' certainly the best bred Man of the party, had none of that general politeness which is so universally pleasing, as his Attentions were entirely confined to Lord Mounteagle.

Sir Walter Raleigh flourished in this & the preceeding reign, & is by many people held in great veneration & respect—But as he was an enemy of the noble Essex, I have nothing to say in praise of him, & must refer all those who may wish to be acquainted with the particulars of his Life, to Mr Sheridan's play of the Critic, where they will find many interesting Anecdotes as well of him as of his freind Sir Christopher Hatton.—. His Majesty was of that amiable disposition which inclines to Freindships, & in such points was possessed of a keener penetration in Discovering Merit than many other people. I once heard an excellent Sharade on a Carpet, of which the subject I am now on reminds me, and as I think it may afford my Readers some Amusement to *find it out,* I shall here take the liberty of presenting it to them.

Sharade

My first is what my second was to King James the 1st, and you tread on my whole.

The principal favourites of his Majesty were Car, who was afterwards created Earl of Somerset and whose name may have some share in the above mentioned Sharade, & George Villiers afterwards Duke of Buckingham. On his Majesty's death he was succeeded by his son Charles.

CHARLES THE 1ST

THIS amiable Monarch seems born to have suffered Misfortunes equal to those of his lovely Grandmother; Misfortunes which he could not deserve since he was her descendant. Never certainly was there before so many detestable Characters at one time in England as in this period of its History; Never were amiable Men so scarce. The number of them throughout the whole Kingdom amounting only to *five*, besides the inhabitants of Oxford who were always loyal to their King & faithful to his interests. The names of this noble five who never forgot the duty of the Subject, or swerved from their attachment to his Majesty, were as follows,—The King himself, ever stedfast in his own support—Archbishop Laud, Earl of Strafford, Viscount Faulkland & Duke of Ormond who were scarcely less strenuous or zealous in the cause. While the Villains of the time would make too long a list to be written or read; I shall therefore content myself with mentioning the leaders of the Gang. Cromwell, Fairfax, Hampden, & Pym may be considered as the original Causers of all the disturbances Distresses & Civil Wars in which England for many years was embroiled. In this reign as well as in that of Elizabeth, I am obliged in spite of my Attachment to the Scotch, to consider them as equally guilty with the generality of the English, since they dared to think differently from their Sovereign, to forget the Adoration which as *Stuarts* it was their Duty to pay them, to rebel against, dethrone & imprison the unfortunate Mary; to oppose, to deceive, and to sell the no less unfortunate Charles. The Events of this Monarch's reign are too numerous for my pen, and indeed the recital of any Events (except what I make myself) is uninteresting to me; my principal reason for undertaking the History of England being to prove the innocence of the Queen of Scotland, which I flatter myself with having effectually done, and to abuse Elizabeth, tho' I am rather fearful of having fallen short in the latter part of my Scheme.—. As therefore it is not my intention to give any particular account of the distresses into which this King was involved through the misconduct & Cruelty of his Parliament, I shall satisfy myself with vindicating him from the Reproach of Arbitrary & tyrannical Government with which he has often been Charged. This, I feel, is not difficult to be done, for with one argument I am certain of satisfying every sensible & well disposed person

whose opinions have been properly guided by a good Education—& this Argue-
ment is that he was a Stuart.

FINIS

Saturday Nov: 26th 1791

A Collection of Letters

To Miss Cooper

COUSIN
Conscious of the Charming Character which in every Country, & every Clime in
Christendom is Cried, Concerning you, with Caution & Care I Commend to your
Charitable Criticism this Clever Collection of Curious Comments, which have been
Carefully Culled, Collected & Classed by your Comical Cousin

THE AUTHOR

A Collection of Letters

Letter the first
From A Mother to her freind

My Children begin now to claim all my attention in a different Manner from that
in which they have been used to receive it, as they are now arrived at that age when
it is necessary for them in some measure to become conversant with the World.
My Augusta is 17 & her Sister scarcely a twelvemonth younger. I flatter myself that
their education has been such as will not disgrace their appearance in the World,
& that *they* will not disgrace their Education I have every reason to beleive. Indeed
they are sweet Girls—. Sensible yet unaffected—Accomplished yet Easy—. Lively
yet Gentle—. As their progress in every thing they have learnt has been always the
same, I am willing to forget the difference of age, and to introduce them together
into Public. This very Evening is fixed on as their first entrée into life, as we are to

drink tea with Mrs Cope & her Daughter. I am glad that we are to meet no one for my Girls sake, as it would be awkward for them to enter too wide a Circle on the very first day. But we shall proceed by degrees—. Tomorrow Mr Stanly's family will drink tea with us, and perhaps the Miss Phillips will meet them. On Tuesday we shall pay Morning-Visits—On Wednesday we are to dine at Westbrook. On Thursday we have Company at home. On Friday we are to be at a private concert at Sir John Wynne's—& on Saturday we expect Miss Dawson to call in the morning,—which will complete my Daughters Introduction into Life. How they will bear so much dissipation I cannot imagine; of their Spirits I have no fear, I only dread their health.

This mighty affair is now happily over, & my Girls *are out*. As the moment approached for our departure, you can have no idea how the sweet Creatures trembled with fear & expectation. Before the Carriage drove to the door, I called them into my dressing-room, & as soon as they were seated thus addressed them. "My dear Girls the moment is now arrived when I am to reap the rewards of all my Anxieties and Labours towards you during your Education. You are this Evening to enter a World in which you will meet with many wonderfull Things; Yet let me warn you against suffering yourselves to be meanly swayed by the Follies & Vices of others, for beleive me my beloved Children that if you do—I shall be very sorry for it." They both assured me that they would ever remember my advice with Gratitude, & follow it with Attention; That they were prepared to find a World full of things to amaze & shock them: but that they trusted their behaviour would never give me reason to repent the Watchful Care with which I had presided over their infancy & formed their Minds—. "With such expectations & such intentions (cried I) I can have nothing to fear from you—& can chearfully conduct you to Mrs Cope's without a fear of your being seduced by her Example or contaminated by her Follies. Come, then my Children (added I) the Carriage is driving to the door, & I will not a moment delay the happiness you are so impatient to enjoy." When we arrived at Warleigh, poor Augusta could hardly breathe, while Margaret was all Life & Rapture. "The long-expected Moment is now arrived (said she) and we shall soon be in the World."— In a few Moments we were in Mrs Cope's parlour—, where with her daughter she sat ready to receive us. I observed with delight the impression my Children made on them—. They were indeed two sweet, elegant-looking Girls, & tho' somewhat abashed from the peculiarity of their Situation, Yet there was an ease in their Manners & Address which could not fail of pleasing—. Imagine my dear Madam how delighted I must have been in beholding as I did, how attentively they observed every object they saw, how disgusted with some Things, how enchanted with others, how astonished at all! On the whole however they returned in raptures with the World, its Inhabitants, & Manners.

YRS EVER—A-F-.

Letter the second
From a Young lady crossed in Love to her freind—

WHY should this last disappointment hang so heavily on my Spirits? Why should I feel it more, why should it wound me deeper than those I have experienced before? Can it be that I have a greater affection for Willoughby than I had for his amiable predecessors? Or is it that our feelings become more acute from being often wounded? I must suppose my dear Belle that this is the Case, since I am not conscious of being more sincerely attached to Willoughby than I was to Neville, Fitzowen, or either of the Crawfords, for all of whom I once felt the most lasting affection that ever warmed a Woman's heart. Tell me then dear Belle why I still sigh when I think of the faithless Edward, or why I weep when I behold his Bride, for too surely this is the case—. My Freinds are all alarmed for me; They fear my declining health; they lament my want of Spirits; they dread the effects of both. In hopes of releiving my Melancholy, by directing my thoughts to other objects, they have invited several of their freinds to spend the Christmas with us. Lady Bridget Dashwood & her Sister-in-Law Miss Jane are expected on Friday; & Colonel Seaton's family will be with us next week. This is all most kindly meant by my Uncle & Cousins; but what can the presence of a dozen indifferent people do to me, but weary & distress me—. I will not finish my Letter till some of our Visitors are arrived.

Friday Evening—

Lady Bridget came this Morning, and with her, her sweet Sister Miss Jane—. Although I have been acquainted with this charming Woman above fifteen years, Yet I never before observed how lovely she is. She is now about 35, & in spite of sickness, Sorrow and Time is more blooming than I ever saw a Girl of 17. I was delighted with her, the moment she entered the house, & she appeared equally pleased with me, attaching herself to me during the remainder of the day. There is something so sweet, so mild in her Countenance, that she seems more than Mortal. Her Conversation is as bewitching as her appearance—; I could not help telling her how much she engaged my Admiration—. —"Oh! Miss Jane" (said I)—and stopped from an inability at the moment of expressing myself as I could wish—"Oh! Miss Jane" (I repeated)—I could not think of words to suit my feelings—She seemed waiting for my Speech—. I was confused—distressed—. My thoughts were bewildered—and I could only add "How do you do?" She saw & felt for my embarrassment & with admirable presence of mind releived me from it by saying—"My dear Sophia be not uneasy at having exposed Yourself—I will turn the Conversation without appearing to notice it." Oh! how I loved her for her kindness! "Do you ride as much as you used to do?" said she—. "I am advised to ride by my Physician, We have delightful

Rides round us, I have a charming horse, am uncommonly fond of the Amuse-ment," replied I quite recovered from my confusion, "& in short I ride a great deal." "You are in the right my Love," said She, Then repeating the following Line which was an extempore & equally adapted to recommend both Riding & Candour—

"Ride where you may, Be Candid where You can," She added, "*I* rode once, but it is many years ago"—She spoke this in so Low & tremulous a Voice, that I was silent—Struck with her Manner of Speaking I could make no reply. "I have not rid-den, continued she fixing her Eyes on my face, since I was married." I was never so surprised—"Married, Ma'am,!" I repeated. "You may well wear that look of aston-ishment, said she, since what I have said must appear improbable to you—Yet nothing is more true than that I once was married."

"Then why are you called Miss Jane?"

"I married, my Sophia without the consent or knowledge of my father—the late Admiral Annesley. It was therefore necessary to keep the secret from him & from every one, till some fortunate opportunity might offer of revealing it—. Such an opportunity alas! was but too soon given in the death of my dear Capt Dashwood—Pardon these tears, continued Miss Jane wiping her Eyes, I owe them to my Husband's Memory, He fell my Sophia, while fighting for his Country in America after a most happy Union of seven years—. My Children, two sweet Boys & a Girl, who had constantly resided with my Father & me, passing with him & with every one as the Children of a Brother (tho' I had ever been an only child) had as yet been the Comforts of my Life. But no sooner had I lossed my Henry, than these sweet Creatures fell sick & died—. Conceive dear Sophia what my feelings must have been when as an Aunt I attended my Children to their early Grave—. My Father did not survive them many weeks—He died, poor Good old Man, happily ignorant to his last hour of my Marriage."

"But did you not own it, & assume his name at your husband's death?"

"No; I could not bring myself to do it; more especially when in my Children, I lost all inducement for doing it. Lady Bridget, and Yourself are the only persons who are in the knowledge of my having ever been either Wife or Mother. As I could not prevail on myself to take the name of Dashwood (a name which after my Hen-ry's death I could never hear without emotion) and as I was conscious of having no right to that of Annesley, I dropt all thoughts of either, & have made it a point of bearing only my Christian one since my Father's death." She paused—"Oh! my dear Miss Jane (said I) how infinitely am I obliged to you for so entertaining a Story! You cannot think how it has diverted me! But have you quite done?"

"I have only to add my dear Sophia, that my Henry's elder Brother dieing about the same time, Lady Bridget became a Widow like myself, and as we had always loved each other in idea from the high Character in which we had ever been spo-ken of, though we had never met, we determined to live together. We wrote to one another on the same subject by the same post, so exactly did our feelings & our

Actions coincide: We both eagerly embraced the proposals we gave & received of becoming one family, and have from that time lived together in the greatest affection."

"And is this all?" said I, "I hope you have not done."

"Indeed I have; and did you ever hear a Story more pathetic?"

"I never did—and it is for that reason it pleases me so much, for when one is unhappy nothing is so delightful to one's sensations as to hear of equal Misery."

"Ah! but my Sophia why *are you* unhappy?"

"Have you not heard Madam of Willoughby's Marriage?" "But my Love why lament *his* perfidy, when you bore so well that of many young Men before?" "Ah! Madam, I was used to it then, but when Willoughby broke his Engagements I had not been dissapointed for half a year." "Poor Girl!" said Miss Jane.

Letter the third
From A young Lady in distress'd Circumstances
to her freind.

———

A FEW days ago I was at a private Ball given by Mr Ashburnham. As my Mother never goes out she entrusted me to the care of Lady Greville who did me the honour of calling for me in her way & of allowing me to sit forwards, which is a favour about which I am very indifferent especially as I know it is considered as confering a great obligation on me. "So Miss Maria (said her Ladyship as she saw me advancing to the door of the Carriage) you seem very smart tonight—*My* poor Girls will appear quite to disadvantage by *you*. I only hope your Mother may not have distressed herself to set *you* off. Have you got a new Gown on?"

"Yes Ma'am," replied I with as much indifference as I could assume.

"Aye, and a fine one too I think—(feeling it, as by her permission I seated myself by her) I dare say it is all very smart—But I must own, for you know I always speak my mind, that I think it was quite a needless peice of expence—Why could not you have worn your old striped one? It is not my way to find fault with people because they are poor, for I always think that they are more to be despised & pitied than blamed for it, especially if they cannot help it, but at the same time I must say that in my opinion your old striped Gown would have been quite fine enough for its wearer—for to tell you the truth (I always speak my mind) I am very much afraid that one half of the people in the room will not know whether you have a Gown on or not—But I suppose you intend to make your fortune tonight—Well, the sooner the better; & I wish you success."

"Indeed Ma'am I have no such intention.—"

"Who ever heard a Young Lady own that she was a Fortune-hunter?" Miss Greville laughed, but I am sure Ellen felt for me.

"Was your Mother gone to bed before you left her?" said her Ladyship.

"Dear Ma'am" said Ellen, "it is but nine o'clock."

"True Ellen, but Candles cost money, and Mrs Williams is too wise to be extravagant."

"She was just sitting down to supper Ma'am."

"And what had she got for Supper?" "I did not observe". "Bread & Cheese I suppose." "I should never wish for a better supper", said Ellen. "You have never any reason" replied her Mother, "as a better is always provided for you." Miss Greville laughed excessively, as she constantly does at her Mother's wit.

Such is the humiliating Situation in which I am forced to appear while riding in her Ladyship's Coach—I dare not be impertinent, as my Mother is always admonishing me to be humble & patient if I wish to make my way in the world. She insists on my accepting every invitation of Lady Greville, or you may be certain that I would never enter either her House, or her Coach, with the disagreable certainty I always have of being abused for my Poverty while I am in them.— When we arrived at Ashburnham, it was nearly ten o'clock, which was an hour and a half later than we were desired to be there; but Lady Greville is too fashionable (or fancies herself to be so) to be punctual. The Dancing however was not begun as they waited for Miss Greville. I had not been long in the room before I was engaged to dance by Mr. Bernard but just as we were going to stand up, he recollected that his Servant had got his white Gloves, & immediately ran out to fetch them. In the mean time the Dancing began & Lady Greville in passing to another room went exactly before me.— She saw me & instantly stopping, said to me though there were several people close to us;

"Hey day, Miss Maria! What cannot you get a partner? Poor Young Lady! I am afraid your new Gown was put on for nothing. But do not despair; perhaps you may get a hop before the Evening is over." So saying, she passed on without hearing my repeated assurance of being engaged, & leaving me very provoked at being so exposed before every one—Mr Bernard however soon returned & by coming to me the moment he entered the room, and leading me to the Dancers, my Character I hope was cleared from the imputation Lady Greville had thrown on it, in the eyes of all the old Ladies who had heard her speech. I soon forgot all my vexations in the pleasure of dancing and of having the most agreable partner in the room. As he is moreover heir to a very large Estate I could see that Lady Greville did not look very well pleased when she found who had been his Choice.— She was determined to mortify me, and accordingly when we were sitting down between the dances, she came to me with *more* than her usual insulting importance attended by Miss Mason and said loud enough to be heard by half the people in the room, "Pray Miss Maria in what way of business was your Grandfather? for Miss Mason & I cannot agree whether he was a Grocer or a Bookbinder" I saw that she wanted to mortify me and was resolved if I possibly could to prevent her seeing that her scheme succeeded. "Neither Madam; he was a Wine Merchant." "Aye, I knew he was in some such low way—He broke did not he?" "I beleive not Ma'am." "Did not he abscond?" "I never heard that he did." "At least he died insolvent?" "I was never told so before." "Why was not your Father as poor as a Rat?" "I fancy not;" "Was not he in the Kings Bench once?" "I never saw him there." *She* gave me *such* a look, & turned away in a great passion; while I was half delighted with myself for my impertinence, & half afraid of being thought too saucy. As Lady Greville was extremely angry with me, she took no further notice of me all the evening, and indeed had I been in favour I should have been equally neglected, as she was got into a party of great folks & she never speaks to me when she can to any one else. Miss Greville was with her Mother's party at Supper, but Ellen preferred staying with the Bernards & me. We had a very pleasant Dance & as Lady G— slept all the way home, I had a very comfortable ride.

The next day while we were at dinner Lady Greville's Coach stopped at the door, for that is the time of day she generally contrives it should. She sent in a message by the Servant to say that "she should not get out but that Miss Maria must come to the Coach-door, as she wanted to speak to her, and that she must make haste & come immediately—" "What an impertinent Message Mama!" said I— "Go Maria—" replied She—Accordingly I went & was obliged to stand there at her Ladyships pleasure though the Wind was extremely high and very cold.

"Why I think Miss Maria you are not quite so smart as you were last night—But I did not come to examine your dress, but to tell you that you may dine with us the day after tomorrow—Not tomorrow, remember, do not come tomorrow, for we expect Lord and Lady Clermont & Sir Thomas Stanley's family—There will be no occasion for your being very fine for I shant send the Carriage—If it rains you may take an umbrella—" I could hardly help laughing at hearing her give me leave to keep myself dry—"and pray remember to be in time, for I shant wait—I hate my Victuals over-done—But you need not come *before* the time—How does your Mother do—? She is at dinner is not she?" "Yes Ma'am we were in the middle of dinner when your Ladyship came." "I am afraid you find it very cold Maria." said Ellen. "Yes, it is an horrible East wind"—said her Mother—"I assure you I can hardly bear the window down—But you are used to be blown about the wind Miss Maria & that is what has made your Complexion so ruddy & coarse. You young Ladies who cannot often ride in a Carriage never mind what weather you trudge in, or how the wind shews your legs. I would not have *my* Girls stand out of doors as you do in such a day as this. But some sort of people have no feelings either of cold or Delicacy—Well, remember that we shall expect you on Thursday at 5 o'clock—You must tell your Maid to come for you at night—There will be no Moon—and you will have an horrid walk home—My Compts to your Mother—I am afraid your dinner will be cold—Drive on—" And away she went, leaving me in a great passion with her as she always does.

MARIA WILLIAMS

Letter the fourth
From a young Lady rather impertinent to her freind.

———

WE dined yesterday with Mr Evelyn where we were introduced to a very agreable looking Girl his cousin. I was extremely pleased with her appearance, for added to the charms of an engaging face, her manner & voice had something peculiarly interesting in them. So much so, that they inspired me with a great curiosity to know the history of her Life, who were her Parents, where she came from, and what had befallen her, for it was then only known that she was a relation of Mrs Evelyn, and that her name was Grenville. In the evening a favourable opportunity offered to me of attempting at least to know what I wished to know, for every one played at Cards but Mrs Evelyn, My Mother, Dr Drayton, Miss Grenville and myself, and as the two former were engaged in a whispering Conversation, & the Doctor fell asleep, we were of necessity obliged to entertain each other. This was what I wished and being determined not to remain in ignorance for want of asking, I began the Conversation in the following Manner.

"Have you been long in Essex Ma'am?"

"I arrived on Tuesday".

"You came from Derbyshire?"

"No Ma'am!" appearing surprised at my question, "from Suffolk." You will think this a good dash of mine my dear Mary, but you will know that I am not wanting for Impudence when I have any end in veiw. "Are you pleased with the Country Miss Grenville? Do you find it equal to the one you have left?"

"Much superior Ma'am in point of Beauty." She sighed. I longed to know for why.

"But the face of any Country however beautiful" said I, "can be but a poor consolation for the loss of one's dearest Freinds." She shook her head, as if she felt the truth of what I said. My Curiosity was so much raised, that I was resolved at any rate to satisfy it.

"You regret having left Suffolk then Miss Grenville?" "Indeed I do." You were born there I suppose?" "Yes Ma'am I was & passed many happy years there—".

"That is a great comfort—said I—I hope Ma'am that you never spent any *un*happy one's there."

"Perfect Felicity is not the property of Mortals, & no one has a right to expect uninterrupted Happiness—*Some* Misfortunes I have certainly met with—."

"*What* Misfortunes dear Ma'am?" replied I, burning with impatience to know every thing. "*None* Ma'am I hope that have been the effect of any wilfull fault in me." "I dare say not Ma'am, & have no doubt but that any sufferings you may have experienced could arise only from the cruelties of Relations or the Errors of Freinds." She sighed—"You seem unhappy my dear Miss Grenville—Is it in my power to soften your Misfortunes." "*Your* power Ma'am replied she extremely surprised; it is in *no ones* power to make me happy." She pronounced these words in so mournfull & solemn an accent, that for some time I had not courage to reply. I was actually silenced. I recovered myself however in a few moments & looking at her with all the affection I could, "My dear Miss Grenville said I, you appear extremely young—& may probably stand in need of some one's advice whose regard for you, joined to superior Age, perhaps superior Judgement might authorise her to give it—. I am that person, & I now challenge you to accept the offer I make you of my Confidence and Freindship, in return to which I shall only ask for yours—."

"You are extremely obliging Ma'am—said She—& I am highly flattered by your attention to me—. But I am in no difficulty, no doubt, no uncertainty of situation in which any Advice can be wanted. Whenever I am however continued she brightening into a complaisant smile, I shall know where to apply."

I bowed, but felt a good deal mortified by such a repulse; Still however I had not given up my point. I found that by the appearance of Sentiment & Freindship nothing was to be gained & determined therefore to renew my Attacks by Questions & Suppositions. "Do you intend staying long in this part of England Miss Grenville?"

"Yes Ma'am, some time I beleive."

"But how will Mr & Mrs Grenville bear your Absence?"

"They are neither of them alive Ma'am."

This was an answer I did not expect—I was quite silenced & never felt so awkward in my Life—.

Letter the fifth
From a Young Lady very much in love to her Freind.

———

My Uncle gets more stingy, my Aunt more particular, & I more in love every day. What shall we all be at this rate by the end of the year! I had this morning the happiness of receiving the following Letter from my dear Musgrove.

Sackville St: Jan:ry 7th

It is a month to day since I beheld my lovely Henrietta, & the sacred anniversary must & shall be kept in a manner becoming the day—by writing to her. Never shall

I forget the moment when her Beauties first broke on my sight—No time as you well know can erase it from my Memory. It was at Lady Scudamores. Happy Lady Scudamore to live within a mile of the divine Henrietta! When the lovely Creature first entered the room, Oh! what were my sensations? The sight of you was like the sight of a wonderful fine Thing. I started—I gazed at her with Admiration—She appeared every moment more Charming, and the unfortunate Musgrove became a Captive to your Charms before I had time to look about me. Yes Madam, I had the happiness of adoring you, an happiness for which I cannot be too grateful. "What said he to himself is Musgrove allowed to die for Henrietta? Enviable Mortal; and may he pine for her who is the object of universal Admiration, who is adored by a Colonel, & toasted by a Baronet! Adorable Henrietta how beautiful you are! I declare you are quite divine! You are more than Mortal. You are an angel. You are Venus herself. In short Madam you are the prettiest Girl I ever saw in my Life—& her beauty is encreased in her Musgroves Eyes, by permitting him to love her & allowing me to hope. And Ah! Angelic Miss Henrietta Heaven is my Witness how ardently I do hope for the death of your villanous Uncle & his Abandoned Wife, Since my fair one will not consent to be mine till their decease has placed her in affluence above what my fortune can procure—. Though it is an improvable Estate—. Cruel Henrietta to persist in such a resolution! I am at present with my Sister where I mean to continue till my own house which tho' an excellent one is at present somewhat out of repair, is ready to receive me. Amiable princess of my Heart farewell—Of that heart which trembles while it signs itself your most ardent Admirer & devoted humble Serv.t.

T. MUSGROVE

There is a pattern for a Love-letter Matilda! Did you ever read such a master-piece of Writing? Such Sense, Such Sentiment, Such purity of Thought, Such flow of Language & such unfeigned Love in one Sheet? No, never I can answer for it, since a Musgrove is not to be met with by every Girl. Oh! how I long to be with him! I intend to send him the following in answer to his Letter tomorrow.

My dearest Musgrove—. Words can not express how happy your Letter made me; I thought I should have cried for Joy, for I love you better than any body in the World. I think you the most amiable, & the handsomest Man in England, & so to be sure you are. I never read so sweet a Letter in my Life. Do write me another just like it, & tell me you are in love with me in every other line. I quite die to see you. How shall we manage to see one another? for we are so much in love that we cannot live asunder. Oh! my dear Musgrove you cannot think how impatiently I wait for the death of my Uncle and Aunt—If they will not die soon, I beleive I shall run mad, for I get more in love with you every day of my Life.

How happy your Sister is to enjoy the pleasure of your Company in her house, and how happy every body in London must be because you are there. I hope you will be so kind as to write to me again soon, for I never read such sweet Letters as yours. I am my dearest Musgrove most truly & faithfully yours for ever & ever. Henrietta Halton

I hope he will like my answer; it is as good a one as I can write, though nothing to his; Indeed I had always heard what a dab he was at a Love-letter. I saw him you know for the first time at Lady Scudamore's—And when I saw her Ladyship afterwards she asked me how I liked her Cousin Musgrove?

"Why upon my word said I, I think he is a very handsome young Man."

"I am glad you think so replied she, for he is distractedly in love with you."

"Law! Lady Scudamore, said I, how can you talk so ridiculously?"

"Nay, t'is very true answered She, I assure you, for he was in love with you from the first moment he beheld you."

"I wish it may be true said I, for that is the only kind of love I would give a far-thing for—There is some Sense in being in love at first sight."

"Well, I give you Joy of your conquest, replied Lady Scudamore, and I beleive it to have been a very complete one; I am sure it is not a contemptible one, for my Cousin is a charming young fellow, has seen a great deal of the World, and writes the best Love-letters I ever read."

This made me very happy, and I was excessively pleased with my conquest. However, I thought it proper to give myself a few Airs—So I said to her—

"This is all very pretty Lady Scudamore, but you know that we young Ladies who are Heiresses must not throw ourselves away upon Men who have no fortune at all."

"My dear Miss Halton said She, I am as much convinced of that as you can be, and I do assure you that I should be the last person to encourage your marrying any one who had not some pretentions to expect a fortune with you. Mr Musgrove is so far from being poor that he has an estate of Several hundreds an year which is capable of great Improvement, and an excellent House, though at present it is not quite in repair."

"If that is the case replied I, I have nothing more to say against him, and if as you say he is an informed young Man and can write good Love-letters, I am sure I have no reason to find fault with him for admiring me, tho' perhaps I may not marry him for all that Lady Scudamore."

"You are certainly under no obligation to marry him answered her Ladyship, except that which love himself will dictate to you, for if I am not greatly mistaken you are at this very moment unknown to yourself, cherishing a most tender affection for him."

"Law, Lady Scudamore replied I blushing how can you think of such a thing?"

"Because every look, every word betrays it, answered She; Come my dear Henrietta, consider me as a friend, and be sincere with me—Do not you prefer Mr Musgrove to any man of your acquaintance?"

"Pray do not ask me such questions Lady Scudamore, said I turning away my head, for it is not fit for me to answer them."

"Nay my Love replied she, now you confirm my suspicions. But why Henrietta should you be ashamed to own a well-placed Love, or why refuse to confide in me?"

"I am not ashamed to own it; said I taking Courage. I do not refuse to confide in you or blush to say that I do love your cousin Mr Musgrove, that I am sincerely attached to him, for it is no disgrace to love a handsome Man. If he were plain indeed I might have had reason to be ashamed of a passion which must have been mean since the Object would have been unworthy. But with such a figure & face, & such beautiful hair as your Cousin has, why should I blush to own that such Superior Merit has made an impression on me."

"My sweet Girl (said Lady Scudamore embracing me with great Affection) what a delicate way of thinking you have in these Matters, and what a quick discernment for one of your years! Oh! how I honour you for such Noble Sentiments!"

"Do you Ma'am? said I; You are vastly obliging. But pray Lady Scudamore did your Cousin himself tell you of his Affection for me? I shall like him the better if he did, for what is a Lover without a Confidante?"

"Oh! my Love replied She, you were born for each other. Every word you say more deeply convinces me that your Minds are actuated by the invisible power of simpathy, for your opinions and Sentiments so exactly coincide. Nay, the colour of your Hair is not very different. Yes my dear Girl, the poor despairing Musgrove did reveal to me the story of his Love—. Nor was I surprised at it—I know not how it was, but I had a kind of presentiment that he *would* be in love with you."

"Well, but how did he break it to you?"

"It was not till after supper. We were sitting round the fire together talking on indifferent subjects, though to say the truth the Conversation was cheifly on my side, for he was thoughtful and silent, when on a sudden he interrupted me in the midst of something I was saying, by exclaiming in a most Theatrical tone—

Yes I'm in love I feel it now

And Henrietta Halton has undone me—"

"Oh! What a Sweet Way replied I, of declaring his Passion! To make such a couple of charming Lines about me! What a pity it is that they are not in rhime!"

"I am very glad you like it, answered She; To be sure there was a great deal of Taste in it. And are you in love with her, Cousin? said I. I am very sorry for it, for unexceptionable as you are in every respect, with a pretty Estate capable of Great improvements, and an excellent House tho' somewhat out of repair, Yet who can hope to aspire with success to the adorable Henrietta who has had an offer from a Colonel & been toasted by a Baronet"—"*That* I have—" cried I. Lady Scudamore continued. "Ah dear Cousin replied he, I am so well convinced of the little Chance I can have of winning her who is adored by thousands, that I need no assurances of yours to make me more thoroughly so. Yet surely neither you or the fair Henrietta herself will deny me the exquisite Gratification of dieing for her, of falling a victim of her Charms. And when I am dead"—continued he—

"Oh Lady Scudamore," said I wiping my eyes, "that such a sweet Creature should talk of dieing!"

"It is an affecting Circumstance indeed," replied Lady Scudamore. "When I am dead said he, Let me be carried & lain at her feet, & perhaps she may not disdain to drop a pitying tear on my poor remains."

"Dear Lady Scudamore interrupted I, say no more on this affecting Subject. I cannot bear it."

"Oh! how I admire the sweet sensibility of your Soul, and as I would not for Worlds wound it too deeply, I will be silent."

"Pray go on," said I. She did so.

"And then added he, Ah! Cousin imagine what my transports will be when I feel the dear precious drops trickle on my face! Who would not die to taste such extacy! And when I am interred, may the divine Henrietta bless some happier Youth with her affection, May he be as tenderly attached to her as the hapless Musgrove & while *he* crumbles to dust, May they live an example of Felicity in the Conjugal state!"

Did you ever hear any thing so pathetic? What a charming wish, to be lain at my feet when he was dead! Oh! what an exalted mind he must have to be capable of such a wish! Lady Scudamore went on.

"Ah! my dear Cousin, replied I to him, such noble behaviour as this, must melt the heart of any Woman however obdurate it may naturally be; and could the divine Henrietta but hear your generous wishes for her happiness, all gentle as is her mind, I have not a doubt but that she would pity your affection & endeavour to return it." "Oh! Cousin answered he, do not endeavour to raise my hopes by such flattering Assurances. No, I cannot hope to please this angel of a Woman, and the only thing which remains for me to do, is to die." "True Love is ever desponding replied I, but *I* my dear Tom will give you even greater hopes of conquering this fair one's heart, than I have yet given you, by assuring you that I watched her with the strictest attention during the whole day, and could plainly discover that she cherishes in her bosom though unknown to herself, a most tender affection for you."

"Dear Lady Scudamore cried I, This is more than I ever knew!"

"Did I not say that it was unknown to yourself? I did not, continued I to him, encourage you by saying this at first, that Surprise might render the pleasure Still Greater." "No Cousin replied he in a languid voice, nothing will convince me that *I* can have touched the heart of Henrietta Halton, and if you are deceived yourself, do not attempt deceiving me." "In short my Love it was the work of some hours for me to persuade the poor despairing Youth that you had really a preference for him; but when at last he could no longer deny the force of my arguments, or discredit what I told him, his transports, his Raptures, his Extacies are beyond my power to describe."

"Oh! the dear Creature, cried I, how passionately he loves me! But dear Lady Scudamore did you tell him that I was totally dependant on my Uncle & Aunt?"

"Yes, I told him every thing."

"And what did he say?"

"He exclaimed with virulence against Uncles & Aunts; Accused the Laws of England for allowing them to possess their Estates when wanted by their Nephews and Neices, and wished *he* were in the House of Commons, that he might reform the Legislature, & rectify all its abuses."

"Oh! the sweet Man! What a spirit he has!" said I.

"He could not flatter himself he added, that the adorable Henrietta would condescend for his sake to resign those Luxuries & that Splendor to which She had been used, and accept only in exchange the Comforts and Elegancies which his limitted Income could afford her, even supposing that his house were in Readiness to receive her. I told him that it could not be expected that she would; it would be doing her an injustice to suppose her capable of giving up the power she now possesses & so nobly uses of doing such extensive Good to the poorer part of her fellow Creatures, merely for the gratification of you and herself."

"To be sure said I, *I* am very Charitable every now and then. And what did Mr Musgrove say to this?"

"He replied that he was under a melancholy Necessity of owning the truth of what I said, and therefore if he should be the happy Creature destined to be the Husband of the Beautiful Henrietta he must bring himself to wait, however impatiently for the fortunate day, when she might be freed from the power of worthless Relations and able to bestow herself on him."

What a noble Creature he is! Oh! Matilda what a fortunate one *I am* who am to be his Wife! My Aunt is calling to me to come & make the pies, So adeiu my dear freind, & beleive me your &c.—H. Halton.

FINIS

Scraps

To Miss Fanny Catherine Austen

MY DEAR NEICE

As I am prevented by the great distance between Rowling and Steventon from superintending Your Education Myself, the care of which will probably on that account devolve on your Father & Mother, I think it is my particular Duty to prevent your feeling as much as possible the want of my personal instructions, by addressing to You on paper my Opinions & Admonitions on the conduct of Young Women, which you will find expressed in the following pages.—

I am my dear Neice

Your affectionate Aunt

THE AUTHOR.

The female philosopher—

A Letter

MY DEAR LOUISA

Your friend Mr Millar called upon us yesterday in his way to Bath, whither he is going for his health; two of his daughters were with him, but the oldest & the three Boys are with their Mother in Sussex. Though you have often told me that Miss Millar was remarkably handsome, you never mentioned anything of her Sisters' beauty; yet they are certainly extremely pretty. I'll give you their description.—Julia is eighteen; with a countenance in which Modesty, Sense & Dignity are happily blended, she has a form which at once presents you with Grace, Elegance & Symmetry. Charlotte who is just Sixteen is shorter than her Sister, and though her figure cannot boast the easy dignity of Julia's, yet it has a pleasing plumpness which is in a different way as estimable. She is fair & her face is expressive sometimes of softness the most bewitching, and at others of Vivacity the most striking. She appears to have infinite wit and a good humour unalterable; her conversation during the half hour they set with us, was replete with humorous Sallies, Bonmots & repartees; while the sensible, the amiable Julia uttered Sentiments of Morality worthy of a heart like her own. Mr Millar appeared to answer the character I had always received of him. My Father met him with that look of Love, that social Shake, & cordial kiss which marked his gladness at beholding an old & valued friend from whom thro' various circumstances he had been separated nearly twenty Years. Mr Millar observed (and very justly too) that many events had befallen each during that interval of time, which gave occasion to the lovely Julia for making most sensible reflections on the many changes in their situation which so long a period had occasioned, on the advantages of some, & the disadvantages of others. From this subject she made a short digression to the instability of human pleasures & the uncertainty of their duration, which led her to observe that all earthly Joys must be imperfect. She was proceeding to illustrate this doctrine by examples from the Lives of great Men when the Carriage came to the Door and the amiable Moralist with her Father & Sister was obliged to depart; but not without a promise of spending five or six months with us on their return. We of course mentioned you, and I assure you that ample Justice was done to your Merits by all. "Louisa Clarke (said I) is in general a very pleasant Girl, yet sometimes her good humour is clouded by Peevishness, Envy & Spite. She neither wants Understanding nor is without some pretensions to Beauty, but these are so very trifling, that the value she sets on her personal charms, & the adoration she expects them to be offered are at once a striking example of her vanity, her pride, & her folly." So said I, & to my opinion everyone added weight by the concurrence of their own.

your affe:te

ARABELLA SMYTHE

The first Act of a Comedy

Characters

Popgun	Maria
Charles	Pistoletta
Postilion	Hostess
Chorus of Ploughboys	Cook
and	&
Strephon	Chloe

Scene—an Inn

Enter Hostess, Charles, Maria & Cook

Host:ss to Maria)	If the gentry in the Lion should want beds, shew them number 9.—
Maria)	Yes Mistress.—
	exit Maria—

Host:ss to Cook)	If their Honours in the Moon ask for the bill of fare give it them.
Cook)	I wull, I wull.—
	exit Cook.
Host:ss to Charles)	If their Ladyships in the Sun ring their Bell—answer it.
Charles)	Yes Madam.—
	Exeunt Severally—.

Scene changes to the Moon, & discovers Popgun & Pistoletta.

Pistol:tta)	Pray papa, how far is it to London?
Popgun)	My Girl, my Darling, my favourite of all my Children, who art the picture of thy poor Mother, who died two months ago, with whom I am going to Town to marry to Strephon, and to whom I mean to bequeath my whole Estate, it wants seven Miles.

Scene changes to the Sun—

Enter Chloe & a chorus of ploughboys.

Chloe)	Where am I? At Hounslow. Where go I? To London—. What to do? To be married—. Unto whom? Unto Strephon. Who is he? A Youth. Then I will Sing a Song.

SONG

I go to Town
And when I come down
I shall be married to Streephon
And that to me will be fun.

Chorus)	Be fun, be fun, be fun, And that to me will be fun.

Enter cook—

Cook)	Here is the bill of fare.
Chloe reads)	2 Ducks, a leg of beef, a stinking partridge, & a tart.— I will have the leg of beef and the partridge.

exit Cook.

And now I will sing another song.

SONG

I am going to have my dinner,
After which I shan't be thinner,
I wish I had here Strephon
For he would carve the partridge
if it should be a tough one.

Chorus)   Tough one, tough one, tough one,
For he would carve the partridge if it should be a tough
one.

Exit Chloe and Chorus.—.

Scene changes to the inside of the Lion.

Enter Strephon & Postilion.

Streph.)   You drove me from Staines to this place, from whence I
mean to go to Town to marry Chloe. How much is your
due?

Post.)   Eighteen pence.

Streph.)   Alas, my friend, I have but a bad guinea with which I mean
to support myself in Town. But I will pawn to you an undirected Letter that I received from Chloe.

Post.)   Sir, I accept your offer.

End of the first Act.—

A Letter from a Young Lady, whose feelings being too Strong for her Judgement led her into the commission of Errors which her Heart disapproved.—

MANY have been the cares & vicissitudes of my past life, my beloved Ellinor, & the only consolation I feel for their bitterness is that on a close examination of my conduct, I am convinced that I have strictly deserved them. I murdered my father at a very early period of my Life, I have since murdered my Mother, and I am now going to murder my Sister. I have changed my religion so often that at present I have not an idea of any left. I have been a perjured witness in every public tryal for these past twelve Years; and I have forged my own will. In short there is scarcely a crime that I have not committed—But I am now going to reform. Colonel Martin of the Horse guards has paid his Addresses to me, & we are to be married in a few days. As there is something singular in our Courtship, I will give you an account of it. Col: Martin is the second son of the late Sir John Martin who died immensely rich, but bequeathing only one hundred thousand pound a piece to his three younger Children, left the bulk of his fortune, about eight Million to the present Sir Thomas. Upon his small pittance the Colonel lived tolerably contented for nearly four months when he took it into his head to determine on getting the whole of his eldest Brother's Estate. A new will was forged & the Colonel produced it in Court—but nobody would swear to it's being the right Will except himself, & he had sworn so much that nobody beleived him. At that moment I happened to be passing by the door of the Court, and was beckoned in by the Judge who told the Colonel that I was a Lady ready to witness anything for the cause of Justice, & advised him to apply to me. In short the Affair was soon adjusted. The Colonel & I swore to its' being the right will, & Sir Thomas has been obliged to resign all his illgotten Wealth. The Colonel in gratitude waited on me the next day with an offer of his hand—. I am now going to murder my Sister.

Yours Ever.
ANNA PARKER.

A Tour through Wales— in a Letter from a young Lady—

MY DEAR CLARA

I HAVE been so long on the ramble that I have not till now had it in my power to thank you for your Letter—. We left our dear home on last Monday month; and proceeded on our tour through Wales, which is a principality contiguous to England

and gives the title to the Prince of Wales. We travelled on horseback by preference. My Mother rode upon our little pony & Fanny & I walked by her side or rather ran, for my Mother is so fond of riding fast that She galloped all the way. You may be sure that we were in a fine perspiration when we came to our place of resting. Fanny has taken a great many Drawings of the Country, which are very beautiful, tho' perhaps not such exact resemblances as might be wished, from their being taken as she ran along. It would astonish you to see all the Shoes we wore out in our Tour. We determined to take a good Stock with us & therefore each took a pair of our own besides those we set off in. However we were obliged to have them both capped & heelpeiced at Carmarthen, & at last when they were quite gone, Mama was so kind as to lend us a pair of blue Sattin Slippers, of which we each took one and hopped home from Hereford delightfully—

I am your ever affectionate
Elizabeth Johnson.

A Tale.

A Gentleman whose family name I shall conceal, bought a small Cottage in Pembrokeshire about two Years ago. This daring Action was suggested to him by his elder Brother who promised to furnish two rooms & a Closet for him, provided he would take a small house near the Borders of an extensive Forest, and about three Miles from the Sea. Wilhelminus gladly accepted the Offer and continued for some time searching after such a retreat when he was one morning agreably releived from his Suspence by reading this advertisement in a Newspaper.

TO BE LETT

A Neat Cottage on the borders of an extensive forest & about three Miles from the Sea. It is ready furnished except two rooms & a Closet.

The delighted Wilhelminus posted away immediately to his brother, and shewed him the advertisement. Robertus congratulated him & sent him in his Carriage to take possession of the Cottage. After travelling for three days & six Nights without Stopping, they arrived at the Forest & following a track which led by it's side down a steep Hill over which ten Rivulets meandered, they reached the Cottage in half an hour. Wilhelminus alighted, and after knocking for some time without receiving any answer or hearing any one stir within, he opened the door which was fastened only by a wooden latch & entered a small room, which he immediately perceived to be one of the two that were unfurnished—From thence he proceeded into a Closet equally bare. A pair of Stairs that went out of it led him into a room above, no less destitute, & these apartments he found composed the whole of the House. He was by no means displeased with this discovery, as he had the comfort of reflecting that he should not be obliged to lay out any thing on furniture himself—. He returned immediately to his Brother, who took him next day to every Shop in Town, & bought what ever was requisite to furnish the two rooms & the Closet. In a few days every thing was completed, and Wilhelminus returned to take possession of the Cottage. Robertus accompanied him, with his Lady and amiable Cecelia & her two lovely Sisters Arabella and Marina to whom Wilhelminus was tenderly attached, and a large number of Attendants—An ordinary Genius might probably have been embarrassed in endeavouring to accomodate so large a party, but Wilhelminus with admirable presence of mind gave order for the immediate erection of two noble Tents in an open Spot in the Forest adjoining to the house. Their Construction was both simple & elegant—A couple of old blankets, each supported by four sticks, gave a striking proof of that taste for Architecture & that happy ease in overcoming difficulties which were some of Wilhelminus's most striking Virtues.

FINIS

End of the Second Volume